PRAISE FOR
THE INTELLIGENT
FUND INVESTOR

"Researchers in behavioural finance have spent decades cataloguing all manner of cognitive biases. For investors, and fund managers, that is only a starting point. Recognizing how these biases influence your behaviour, and sidestepping them, is the key to better investment decision-making. Wiggins does this and more in his blog and new book, *The Intelligent Fund Investor*."

—Tadas Viskanta, founder and editor of Abnormal Returns and director of investor education at Ritholtz Wealth Management

"Joe's continuous insights on behavioural finance and investor psychology lay the groundwork on ways investors can control their emotions and position themselves for success in investing. There is no doubt that professional and retail investors can learn, grow and become better long-term investors by reading Joe's work."

—Justin Carbonneau, partner at Validea Capital and co-host of the Excess Returns Podcast

"Joe writes with great clarity about the biggest obstacle to investors achieving their financial goals – their own behaviour. His advice is suitable for individual and institutional investors alike and is in stark contrast to the efforts of most financial writing, which tries to predict a future that is inherently unknowable."

—Simon Hallett, former chief investment officer of Harding Loevner and chairman of Plymouth Argyle football club

"Joe's observations about both portfolio manager and underlying investor behaviour are astute, important, and thought-provoking."

—**Clare Flynn Levy, founder and chief executive officer of Essentia Analytics**

"A natural contrarian, keen to challenge the established wisdom of the crowd, Joe is a breath of fresh air to the manager selection community. Building on the foundations of his extensive manager selection experience for market leading investment firms, his behavioural research and insights can help both amateur and professional fund investors avoid becoming their own worst enemies in achieving their goals."

—**James Millard, chief investment officer of Hiscox**

"If you are looking for common sense, look no further than Joe Wiggins. A student of behavioural economics and human heuristics, his thoughts and observations are frequently amongst the most insightful, and useful, I read in markets today. Well worth your time."

—**Nick Kirrage, co-head of the global value team at Schroders**

"Joe Wiggins knows more about the behavioural aspects of investing and asset management than almost any other financial practitioner in the UK. One of the reasons he understands it so well is that he's seen at first hand the problems that behavioural biases cause investors – and that includes professionals, as well as the rest of us. Joe combines that expertise with a lucid and engaging writing style. I can highly recommend this book."

—**Robin Powell, co-author of *Invest Your Way to Financial Freedom***

"One of the oft overlooked keys to successful investment is the ability to control the behavioural biases and weaknesses in decision making to which we are all vulnerable. Joe does an excellent job of explaining the challenges faced by investors and draws on his own experience as a professional investor to suggest ways of addressing these challenges. His writing is always engaging, insightful, and grounded in the real world of investing."

—**Dan Kemp, global chief investment officer at Morningstar Investment Management**

THE
INTELLIGENT
FUND
INVESTOR

Every owner of a physical copy of this edition of

THE INTELLIGENT FUND INVESTOR

can download the eBook for free direct from us at Harriman House, in a DRM-free format that can be read on any eReader, tablet or smartphone.

Simply head to:

ebooks.harriman-house.com/intelligentfundinvestor

to get your copy now.

THE INTELLIGENT FUND INVESTOR

Practical steps for better
results in active and
passive funds

JOE WIGGINS

Harriman
House

HARRIMAN HOUSE LTD
3 Viceroy Court
Bedford Road
Petersfield
Hampshire
GU32 3LJ
GREAT BRITAIN
Tel: +44 (0)1730 233870

Email: enquiries@harriman-house.com
Website: harriman.house

First published in 2022.

Paperback ISBN: 978-0-85719-876-1
eBook ISBN: 978-0-85719-877-8

British Library Cataloguing in Publication Data
A CIP catalogue record for this book can be obtained from the British Library.

For

*Natalie, the best person
I have ever met.*

*Elliott and Lottie,
I hope you turn out to
be just like your mum.*

CONTENTS

INTRODUCTION

I WASN'T SURE I was in the right place. I was driving around a bleak business park in Oxford, far from the renowned university's dreaming spires, looking for the office where I had an early morning meeting.

Then I noticed it.

Parked across two spaces in among the rows of humdrum vehicles was a supercar. A Ferrari. Not in the classic, unmistakable red, but still wonderfully incongruous. In that instant I knew I had reached my destination: the new workplace of Britain's most famous fund manager, Neil Woodford.

Woodford was Britain's answer to Warren Buffett. Labelled by the BBC as "the man who cannot stop making money," he enjoyed incredible success at asset management firm Invesco Perpetual.[1] Adroitly navigating both the dotcom bubble and Global Financial Crisis, he delivered returns materially ahead of the broad stock market. With an ardent following, he came to be regarded as one of the greatest investors of his generation.

In 2014 Woodford shocked the industry. He left behind the £33 billion of assets he managed at Invesco Perpetual to launch an eponymous asset management firm. He wanted to run money free from the constraints and confines of a large company.

Investors followed in their droves. Why wouldn't they? Woodford had proved his pedigree over decades. His new business was an immediate and staggering success. At its peak he managed more than £15bn.

My journey to Oxfordshire to visit Woodford came shortly after the launch of his business. I was tasked with reviewing the prospects of his new fund. I had known Woodford for several years through my role carrying out research on active fund managers. We had enjoyed a somewhat fraught relationship, as he wasn't overly keen on having his decision making scrutinised. He did, however, become more amenable to questioning when seeking to raise money for his fledgling venture.

Following our meeting, I decided not to invest money with Woodford. For a period that appeared to be a foolish decision, as he continued to deliver the type of results upon which he had forged his reputation at his previous employer. Yet those initial successes belied the fact that the foundations were being laid for his stunning downfall.

Within five years of my trip, Woodford's company had been closed. Not only had investors endured heavy losses, but many found themselves locked into the firm's flagship fund and unable to retrieve their cash, despite it supposedly offering daily access.

The Woodford saga is an unpleasant reminder of how difficult fund investing is. Investors entrusted their savings with a man who had served them well for decades, yet it ended in disaster.

But this isn't a book about the travails of an individual fund manager. It is about the flawed beliefs we hold about fund investing, the costly mistakes they lead to and how we can avoid them.

It is about how we can be better fund investors.

The mutual fund industry is a sprawling behemoth. At the end of 2020 there were 126,000 regulated funds registered worldwide, holding assets worth more than $63 trillion. Its growth has provided huge benefits to all types of investors, affording most people the opportunity to access diversified and professionally managed investments.

The universe of investors in funds spans those who will not even realise that they own them – but do so through services such as a workplace pension scheme – to professionals whose job it is to identify the most compelling funds from the staggering array of options.

Most of us are fund investors.

Funds allow us to invest across a vast range of different asset classes and types of investment. From simple, passive, index funds that replicate the returns of a given stock market, to far more complex hedge funds and esoteric vehicles investing in fine wine and art. Virtually any type of investment we care to make can be accessed through a fund.

Although the breadth of choice appears to be an advantage, it is in fact a curse. It makes the job of a fund investor incredibly challenging. We must filter the extensive list of available funds, identify those that are suitable for our objectives, and then judge when to buy and sell.

Fund investing is a decision-making nightmare, and our poor choices have damaging financial consequences.

Is there anything we can do to improve the situation? Absolutely. As I will show, we can transform our fund investing beliefs and behaviours.

I have written this book to help you do just that.

Each of the following chapters focuses on a particular aspect of fund investing. I show why certain beliefs we hold are deeply flawed, answer the key questions facing fund investors and offer guidance on how we can tackle these issues with a different mindset and approach.

Chapter 1 looks at our fascination with star fund managers and why investing with celebrity investors often ends in tears.

Chapter 2 assesses the growth of the index fund industry and why a market cap, passive approach to investing may not be as foolproof as many now believe.

Chapter 3 argues that smooth fund performance should be feared, not sought after.

Chapter 4 highlights the risk inherent in complex funds and shows why investors should not invest in things they do not understand.

Chapter 5 explains why good stories lead to bad investments.

Chapter 6 contends that fund investors should be less concerned about volatility as a measure of risk, but instead focus on the spectre of disaster and disappointment.

Chapter 7 argues that the most popular reason for buying and selling a fund – its past performance – is the worst possible way to make a decision.

Chapter 8 shows how asset managers are rarely aligned with their investors, and why performance fees do not solve this problem.

Chapter 9 makes the case that a long-term approach is an investment advantage available to us all, but few use it.

Chapter 10 seeks to bust the myths surrounding the growth in ESG investing and highlight its true value.

At the close of each chapter there is a ten-point checklist focusing on the key lessons we can apply. This means that across the book there are 100 practical tips to help us make better fund investment decisions.

I will shortly return to the story of Neil Woodford and the problems of star fund managers but, before that, let's explore why fund investing is such a difficult decision-making challenge.

PROLOGUE:
IT'S A MATTER OF BELIEFS
AND BEHAVIOUR

THERE ARE CERTAIN types of decisions that are easy to make, where we know exactly what we want and have a small, clearly defined range of options to select from. This situation could not be further removed from the choices fund investors have to make. Fund investing is a fiendishly difficult decision-making problem.

But what makes it so tough?

There are three main features that prevent fund investors from making good decisions:

1. Too much choice

The sheer scale of the fund universe renders it staggeringly difficult to navigate. In the UK alone, the Investment Association lists over 4,000 funds. By way of context, there are around 600 companies listed on the UK's main stock market index – the FTSE All-Share. Each of the available funds will have different approaches, objectives, performance track records and fee levels. We somehow must decide which is most suitable.

2. Too difficult

It is not only the scale of the opportunity set that makes fund investing so challenging but also the difficulty. How do we assess what the best options available to us are? Our instinct is to look at past performance and choose those with a history of strong returns, or to invest with a popular, high-profile, star fund manager. Both approaches – while common – are highly problematic and often damaging.

Even professional fund investors, who spend months researching individual funds, would not be able to agree on which are the most important aspects to consider when selecting a fund: is it cost, is it manager experience, is it performance, or something else? There is no blueprint or guide. We have an enormous list of potential funds to invest in but no obvious means of effectively filtering it.

3. Too noisy

The final element of the trifecta is noise. We can think of noise as factors that influence our fund selection behaviour but really should not. The most prominent of these is the short-term fluctuations of financial markets and economies, and the stories we tell about them. We cannot predict the movements of stock markets and are terrible at making economic forecasts, but we often let these factors overwhelm our decision making. Markets are in a constant state of flux and change, which means we are easily tempted into injudicious and unnecessary activity.

There are too many funds to choose from, we don't know the most important criteria, and we are easily distracted by things that don't matter. This is a potent cocktail for painful and costly investment mistakes.

The list of errors that we make as fund investors is considerable:

- We buy funds at the peak of their performance and sell laggards at their trough.

- We invest in thematic funds because they are holding the current flavour of the month areas of the stock market.

- We dispose of our riskiest funds during a recession, after they have already fallen severely.

- We are attracted to complex funds we cannot hope to understand because of the fanciful promise of high and smooth returns.

I could continue.

What can we do about it?

One answer would be to invest only in passive, index funds, which track the performance of a particular market, usually at a low cost.

While index funds are a great option for many investors, they are no panacea. Using index funds does not abrogate our responsibility to make investment decisions or remove the potential for harmful errors. Index fund investors still must decide upon the correct markets, the right funds and at the appropriate mix. They will suffer the same dangerous temptations as active fund investors – for instance: "Why am I wasting my time investing in emerging market equities, when the US market has performed so much better?"

All three of the central problems of fund investing – choice, difficulty and noise – apply to index fund investors. There are also some broader misconceptions held about the efficacy of index fund investing that we will explore in Chapter 2.

But if index funds don't remove all of the major decision-making hurdles faced by fund investors, what else can we do?

We can change our beliefs and behaviours.

Nothing can help us more than discarding the flawed but prevalent beliefs held about fund investing that lead to consistently poor decisions.

By shifting our beliefs, we can genuinely strive for better returns and less risk.

———

I have worked in fund research and investment since 2004. Unlike many in the industry claim, I wasn't reading the *Financial Times* at four years old or buying my first company share at six. Instead, I fell into a career in finance. Having no clue what I wanted to do with my life, I applied for many things and was offered a job at a small fund brokerage firm. It was randomness and chance, rather than design. I had little clue what a fund was when I was starting my working life.

Having the opportunity to begin a career in fund research was fortuitous because I had always been fascinated by the behaviour of people. I even studied Sociology at undergraduate level, a fact that often receives quizzical and sceptical looks when mentioned. Yet if the fund industry is about anything it is about people: the managers that run funds, the salespeople that market them and the investors that buy them. Financial markets and economies are a function of the behaviour of groups and individuals. Among the economic models, formulas and forecasts, it is easy to forget the people.

As my career progressed, I found that I was interested in different things to my colleagues and peers. They might worry about the next release of Chinese GDP data or the performance of a particular fund, whereas I was thinking about how I and others made decisions. I was thinking about behaviour.

What made us make the fund investment decisions we did?

To better understand and improve my own decision making, I completed a Master's in Behavioural Science at the London School of Economics in 2017. This was crucial to me developing a broader understanding of our behavioural inconsistencies and applying it to fund investing in a more formal and disciplined manner. Shortly after completing my studies I started a blog (behaviouralinvestment. com) which focused on employing behavioural science to investment decision making.

Given my background, this could easily have been a book about behavioural biases. A taxonomy of our most damaging behavioural mistakes and what to do about them. Unfortunately, this just would not work. The investing world and our behaviour are simply too messy and complicated. Many of the main behavioural biases that have been identified are harmful in some situations but not in others.

There are biases that have the exact opposite impact to each other, and many that only apply in very narrow contexts.

Let's take some common examples:

- **Loss aversion**

  Loss aversion means that we suffer the pain of a loss more keenly than we enjoy a commensurate gain. This can lead to us taking too little risk in our investments because of the fear of temporary losses, which can be incredibly costly for long-term investors. However, loss aversion can also be beneficial. It can help us avoid situations where we invest in very high-risk investments with the potential for catastrophic losses such as concentrated and leveraged funds.

- **Status quo bias / action bias**

  Status quo bias is about our tendency to stick with what we have; action bias is our predilection for action over inaction. So, which is it? It depends!

- **Disposition effect**

  The disposition effect is an investor preference for selling winning positions, while holding on to losers. An opposite effect has been identified that applies only to fund investors – the aptly named reverse disposition effect. Investors in funds are more likely to hold strongly performing funds and sell losers.[1] This difference is because fund investors have someone else to blame for poor returns (the fund manager), and so are happier to sell the laggards!

Do investors suffer from behavioural biases? Absolutely. Many of them will be covered in the chapters ahead. But biases are consistent and our investing behaviour is erratic, noisy and context dependent. A list of biases would not be sufficient or effective.

This is a book about beliefs, not just biases.

Our beliefs about fund investing lead us to make poor investment decisions and compromise our long-term outcomes. Many of these are informed by our biases, but they are much more. The beliefs we hold are the lens through which we view the world, and they dominate our fund investment decisions.

CHAPTER 1

DON'T INVEST IN STAR FUND MANAGERS

ONE OF THE greatest temptations for fund investors is to invest with a star fund manager. Amid the immense universe of funds, the impressive track record and high profile of star managers can make them look like an obvious choice.

The purpose of this chapter is to show why this is not a good idea. Indeed, I would go as far as to suggest we should never invest with a star manager.

What is the problem here? And how do we avoid making this mistake?

Although the challenges faced by each star fund manager are distinct, they do share some common features. These are:

- A substantial growth in assets under management impairing the investment process.

- A misalignment of interests between the fund manager and their investors.

- Increasing incidence of hubris and the manager operating outside of their circle of competence.

- A lack of adequate independent challenge or control.

I discuss these problems in this chapter.

Let's start by returning to the story of one of the most spectacular fund manager demises in recent investing history. As we will see, this tale is instructive on the risks of investing with star managers.

Why did Britain's star fund manager fail?

Many high-profile fund managers have seen their reputations tarnished by prolonged periods of poor performance. But Neil Woodford's decline was more dramatic and pernicious.

The roots were in his predilection for investing in small, unquoted companies, often involved in biotechnology – think one laboratory hoping to develop the next blockbuster drug. These companies were usually the domain of venture capital investors rather than mainstream investment funds held by the wider public. Although offering potentially huge gains, small, unquoted companies are typically speculative and, as they are not listed on the stock market, incredibly difficult to value and trade.

Woodford had long been interested in this type of company. They featured in the funds he managed at Invesco Perpetual. The greater freedom afforded to him at his new business meant that these companies became a far more prominent feature of his investment approach.

Aside from their speculative nature, there was another major problem with Woodford's small, unquoted investments. The funds that Woodford was managing were daily dealing, meaning that investors were free to redeem their holding on any given day. This was jarringly incompatible with his fund's increasing exposure to these illiquid securities, which could take weeks, months or even years to sell.

Woodford had created a classic liquidity mismatch between the terms offered to investors and the underlying assets he held.

Just like a bank run, an underlying liquidity problem in an investment fund can be ignored or obscured during the good times – when performance is strong and investors continue to put in new money. But a change in sentiment can lead to the situation turning sour with alarming speed. The catalyst for Woodford's problems was a period of unusually weak performance. This inevitably led to disappointed investors withdrawing money from his funds.

It is the rapid removal of money that leads to the realisation of hidden or neglected liquidity risks. To manage large and increasing outflows, Woodford had to sell down the more liquid, stock market listed companies in his portfolio. This resulted in a sharp increase in the hard to sell unquoted element. Not because he was buying more of these companies – but because as he sold his positions in larger, listed names, the less liquid element became a greater proportion of the portfolio. This led to an eventual breach of the regulations around the exposure to such companies in a public investment fund.[1]

Woodford's high profile exacerbated the situation. The intense media coverage precipitated ever-increasing outflows and eventually resulted in the fund being suspended, meaning that investors could no longer access their money.

In an unprecedented step, the authorised corporate director of Woodford's funds (a type of trustee responsible for independent oversight) sacked him as manager of his own funds – a unique type of ignominy. This ultimately led to the business being wound down five years after its much-vaunted launch. While Woodford's company was wildly profitable over its short lifespan, investors were left nursing severe losses and unable to withdraw their money.

How do we avoid investing in situations like Woodford?

To prevent becoming embroiled in situations such as that suffered by Woodford, we could perform forensic analysis on each fund manager and attempt to decipher the many imponderables to judge future return prospects and risks. The far easier option is to stop investing in star fund managers and the unique set of problems they bring with them.

There is no precise definition of a star fund manager, but features such as having an inescapable media presence, being known by individuals outside of the investment industry (if someone who doesn't know anything about investing has heard of them, we should start to worry), and running a sizeable amount of money are common.

We might regard the Woodford catastrophe as an idiosyncratic issue about the travails of a particular individual, but this would be a mistake. There are broad and critical lessons we can all learn.

Does a larger fund mean lower returns and higher risk?

> It's a huge structural advantage not to have a lot of money. I think I could make you 50% a year on $1 million. No, I know I could. I guarantee that.
>
> **–Warren Buffett**

By definition, a star fund manager has been successful and is well known. This combination will inevitably mean they have attracted a significant pot of money to manage. Whatever the size of the funds, most asset management companies will tell you that there are "no capacity issues" – meaning that the investment approach of their most important fund manager is unaffected by the amount of money they invest.

This nonsensical view highlights the inherent conflict faced by all asset management companies. Their profitability is largely driven by the fees they charge on assets under management. The more money they run, the greater their revenues. Yet as assets grow, the ability of their fund managers to add value diminishes.

Given that the incentivisation of most fund managers and asset management executives is driven by the operational performance of the business, the profit motive typically wins out. An asset manager closing one of their largest and most popular funds is akin to Apple announcing to shareholders that they no longer wish to sell iPhones as the business is profitable enough already. The asset manager will obviously be reluctant to do it and so, of course, they say that fund size is not a problem.

Unfortunately, it is inescapable that a fund manager running an increasing amount of money faces challenges with both the size of opportunity set and liquidity.

The problems of fund size

Imagine you are a young fund manager. You have been working as an analyst and have now been handed a £100m portfolio of UK equities to manage. You want to run a portfolio of 33 stocks, with each stock having an equal weighting. Your average investment in any company will be £3m. At the time of writing, the median market capitalisation of a company on the FTSE All-Share was £1.4bn, meaning that a typical position will see you own just 0.2% of any company. Not a size that should present any problems in trading the stock.

Now imagine you are an experienced fund manager. You forged your reputation in the last bear market and delivered stellar outperformance. Your success and the publicity around it has resulted in your fund growing in size to £10bn. You aim to run an equally weighted portfolio of 33 stocks. Given this, your average investment in a company is a staggering £303m; you would own 22% of the median FTSE All-Share company.

As fund size grows, the opportunity set erodes. Of the 412 companies with a market capitalisation over £100m on the FTSE All-Share (excluding investment trusts), a 3% position in your fund would lead to ownership of more than 10% of the company in 284 instances, and more than 30% in 175 cases.

A stake over 30% means you are formally required to launch a takeover bid for the entire firm. While this rule does not apply to investment funds, this gives an indication of the magnitude and materiality of the positions you are now forced to take.

If company ownership is limited to 10% and we run an equally weighted portfolio of 33 stocks, here is how our investable universe shrinks as fund size grows.

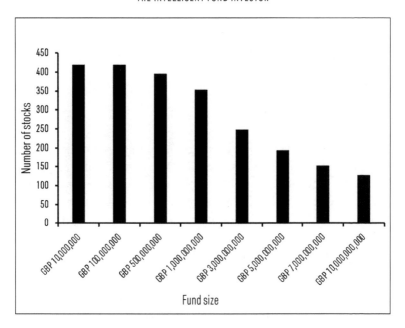

As the quantum of money we run grows, the number of companies we have to choose from reduces dramatically. The more successful we are, the harder our job becomes.

Not only is it increasingly difficult to access attractive investment ideas, buying and selling companies becomes incredibly challenging.

Asset growth increases illiquidity and inflexibility

Size of assets not only restricts the range of opportunities available to a fund manager – it also fosters material liquidity risks and stymies flexibility. This is best portrayed with an example.

The median stock in the FTSE All-Share – based on size – is Capital & Counties Properties. This is a property developer with a market capitalisation of £1.4bn. If running the £10bn fund detailed earlier, a £303m stake would entail owning over 22% of the company. To sell this position in its entirety – participating in 20% of the average daily volume traded – would take over 200 days!

It would be possible to exit the position more swiftly, but not without materially impacting the share price. This type of situation leaves a large fund incredibly vulnerable to clients withdrawing money. A fund manager can either attempt to sell less liquid positions at great cost, or sell more liquid holdings, but see the illiquid element increase as a proportion of the portfolio. Just as happened with Woodford.

Even absent outflows, a fund manager with large assets becomes inherently inflexible. If something changes at Capital & Counties, or a better opportunity emerges elsewhere, the speed at which the manager can scale back or entirely remove the position is severely impaired.

The notion that a successful fund manager is not compromised by an increasing fund size is entirely spurious. To maintain their approach they are forced to either assume far greater liquidity risk and inflexibility (because trading becomes so difficult, costly and laborious), or change what they do – buying an increasing list of companies or investing in different areas. Each of these options involves the manager diverging from what made them successful and leaves investors exposed to a multitude of risks.

The time to invest in a star manager is before they have attained such status; when they had the freedom of running a far smaller pot of money. Unfortunately, we cannot help but believe that strong past performance can persist indefinitely.

Why won't strong past performance persist?

> It's stupid the way people are extrapolating the past.
> And not slightly stupid, massively stupid.
>
> **–Charlie Munger**

Why is it that we are so prone to accept the biased assurances of asset managers and assume that a star fund manager can maintain their track record of success?

One reason is simple availability. As stories of the manager's success become more common, we are more likely to become aware of them

Another is our desire to herd. We see other people successfully making money with a manager and we don't want to miss out.

But more than anything else it is about the lure of past performance. Past performance overwhelms all other considerations and we are fooled into believing that it can go on forever. Even if that is an impossibility.

Sometimes history cannot repeat itself

During the 2001 Berkshire Hathaway Shareholder Meeting, Warren Buffett and Charlie Munger were asked a question about how they could deliver a 15% earnings growth rate in their underlying companies, to which Buffett replied:

> Well, I think the probability of us achieving 15 percent growth in earnings over an extended period of years is so close to zero, it's not worth calculating.

Between 1965 and the end of 2000, the average annual gain in the per share market value of Berkshire Hathaway was 33%. Was it entirely unreasonable for the questioner to enquire about future earnings growth of 15%? And, given his track record, why was Buffett so unequivocal in his view that it could not be achieved?

Buffett knew two things. First, the prior success of Berkshire Hathaway meant that its vast scale had dramatically reduced its opportunity set. There are not many companies delivering 15% earnings growth, and certainly few large companies achieve that. Second, excess growth at scale becomes a mathematical impossibility. If a large company can grow earnings at 15% while the overall economy grows at 5%, then in time the company will become the economy. Sooner or later the company's growth must slow.

This has been the case for Berkshire Hathaway. From 2001 to 2021, the average annual gain in market value fell to below 10%.

Yet these inconveniences are easily ignored. The questioner at the shareholder meeting was not thinking about the mathematical reality of delivering such high levels of growth. They were focused on the past track record of Munger and Buffett. Surely there was nothing to stop the two most renowned investors of their generation (perhaps in history) maintaining the tremendous results they had delivered in the past?

Why do we extrapolate?

Extrapolation – assuming that past performance will continue into the future – is a convenient mental shortcut. It avoids us having to get lost in a quagmire of complexity and uncertainty.

It is also psychologically comfortable. Imagine claiming that the historic results of a particular star manager are unsustainable. You will be taking a contrarian stance against conventional wisdom and a track record. It is far easier and safer to assume that the performance will persist.

In the same shareholder meeting in 2001, Munger commented on the extrapolation problem in relation to the fanciful levels of future returns expected by pension funds. He said:

> It's part of the human condition that people extrapolate the recent past. And so, since returns from common stocks have been high for quite a long period, they extrapolate that they will continue to be very high into the future.

The returns produced by star fund managers have almost inevitably been abnormally strong in the past. That's why they are star managers! As Munger suggests, we seem inherently disposed to believing that this pattern will continue.

Unfortunately, it will not.

It is not just asset size (as we saw previously) that creates an extrapolation problem for return expectations of star fund managers. There are myriad other reasons why it is naïve to assume that their form will persist.

The most dangerous situations are where a fund manager gets one big call right and dines out on it for the rest of their career. They might even have books or films produced about them. In such cases we extrapolate from a single but incredibly salient period.

Even if a manager has built their reputation in a more measured fashion – delivering consistent outperformance for a sustained period and maintaining a stable investment approach – extrapolation can still be incredibly damaging.

This could be because the environment changes and their style is no longer effective. Or simply because their exceptional historic performance is now reflected in the price and valuations of the securities in which they invest. To repeat their historic feats they will need to do something different. Doing something different is almost always a recipe for trouble, as we shall see later in the chapter.

We could also simply be investing with a manager who has struck it lucky in the past. Even if not a single fund manager had investing skill, there would be those who produced outperformance. If we get enough people flipping coins, someone will get ten heads in a row. It doesn't mean we should bankroll their trip to Las Vegas. We cannot help but see patterns and construct stories out of random outcomes. Although difficult to accept, our star fund manager might simply have been fortunate rather than good.

Despite a high level of assets and strong historic performance being a recipe for poor future returns for a star fund manager, this doesn't mean that the manager has to suffer. In most cases it is the investors who get the rough side of the deal.

Why do fund managers make money when we don't?

In the final year before his company's closure, Neil Woodford and his partner, Craig Newman, received £13.8m in dividends.[2] This was despite the losses registered by their funds and the inability of clients to withdraw their money.

This asymmetry of risk – heads I win, tails you lose – is an embedded feature of the asset management industry. Fund managers are commonly rewarded handsomely, no matter their performance. Although the manager bears some risk in this relationship (they could be fired by their employer if their performance is sub-par), the arrangement is horribly skewed in their favour. This imbalance is especially pronounced when it comes to star fund managers.

When a fund manager has been successful and reached star status, we can be certain of one of two things. They have either entered into a revenue share agreement, meaning they directly receive a portion of the management fees for the funds they manage. Or (as in the case of Woodford), they have started their own enterprise to personally realise all the value in the brand they have developed. In either scenario the individual will be richly remunerated simply because of the scale of the assets being managed and irrespective of the results they deliver for their clients.

Who suffers the consequences of our actions?

The problems inherent in this type of risk asymmetry, and its impact on behaviour, is the cornerstone of Nassim Nicholas Taleb's book *Skin in the Game*.[3] As an example of an equitable division of risk, Taleb cites Hammurabi's Code, a set of 282 laws set out by King Hammurabi of Babylon, Mesopotamia, around 4,000 years ago. A rule on building construction is particularly pertinent when considering the problem of risk asymmetry. It stated:

> If a builder builds a house for a man and does not make its construction firm, and the house which he has built collapses and causes the death of the owner of the house, that builder shall be put to death.

This is a perfect, if somewhat extreme, example of a structure that imbues accountability and ensures that the incentives of the service provider are aligned with the recipient. Asset management is some distance from such an equitable situation.

It is not that a star fund manager isn't incentivised to generate outperformance (they will garner more assets and fees if they do), but that outperformance is not required for them to be extraordinarily well remunerated. Furthermore, and perhaps most crucially, if a star manager's endeavours end in disaster through negligence or bad luck, the majority of the cost is borne by us. Although the star fund manager's future earnings potential may be dimmed if they are fired, or their reputation tarnished, their past earnings are unaffected.

Thus, there is a situation where the ascent of a fund manager to star status sees their incentives become increasingly misaligned with the clients for whom they manage money.

Yet it is not simply that clients end up bearing risk that the fund managers do not. It's also the case that a star fund manager is more likely to expose their investors to new risks.

Should fund managers stick to what they know?

If you are a star fund manager, you have likely delivered phenomenal performance for the funds that you manage. Your success has meant that you have become a vital part of the profitability of the business that you work for, which affords you incredible power and influence within the organisation. You might make frequent media appearances and be asked to opine on issues well outside your narrow area of expertise. You enjoy the adulation and your burgeoning importance, and feel it is just reward for your accomplishments.

Receiving constant reminders of your own brilliance undoubtedly feels good, but it can have catastrophic consequences, for you and others. Just ask Napoleon.

Before embarking on his disastrous campaign in Russia in 1812, Napoleon was Emperor of the French, King of Italy and the dominant presence across the European continent. He commanded a 685,000 strong army and had won 35 of his 38 battles. Unfortunately for him, these factors could not prevent over 400,000 French casualties and a defeat in Russia which laid the foundations for the iconic leader's exile to the island of Elba.

In a paper written in 2000, a group of academics specialising in research on executive leadership used Napoleon's failure in Russia as a salutary lesson on the dangers of hubris and the problematic behaviours that can stem from holding an exaggerated sense of one's own ability and importance.[4] They contended that one of the key drivers in the development of hubris is frequent and consistent success:

Narcissism and hubris feed on further successes. As an executive accumulates a record of accomplishment, his or her susceptibility to hubris tends to grow. Indeed, a consistent theme that runs through the various accounts of Napoleon's career is the inclination for his narcissism and hubris to grow with each successful campaign.

By definition, a fund manager's star reputation is forged on early successes, and these achievements typically serve to foster ever-increasing self-belief and ambition. As Napoleon remarked following victory in Italy: "They haven't seen anything yet, and the future holds successes far beyond what we have so far accomplished."

The downside of self-confidence

Confidence is a richly valued trait in a fund manager. It is perceived to be a necessary characteristic to adopt the anti-consensus views required to beat the market. Yet it should serve more as a caution than an accolade. The excessive self-confidence, so often a trait of prominent fund managers, can lead to the assumption of undue risks. These risks arise when individuals step outside their circle of competence.

Although Warren Buffett is lauded as a great investor, this is a broad and meaningless label. The term is far too nebulous. The crucial question – and one which often gets lost – is: great at what, exactly? This is an issue that Buffett directly addressed himself when he said:

> Everybody's got a different circle of competence. The important thing is not how big the circle is. The important thing is staying inside the circle.

Even if a fund manager has generated outstanding returns through the application of skill – and, as we have seen, we can never be sure that it wasn't simply luck – it is almost certain that the skill exhibited is narrowly confined to a specific domain.

Warren Buffett's ability to identify companies that could sustain high returns on capital does not mean that he has particularly valuable insights on when the US economy will next enter a recession, or any other of a million different things. Buffett has always been clear about his edge. Other star fund managers, likely giddy from success and adulation, have been tempted to step far away from the areas that made them successful in the first place.

Woodford is not an exception

Neil Woodford's increasing predilection for investing in tiny, specialised and complex biotechnology companies could not have been further removed from the large tobacco and pharmaceutical stocks on which he forged his reputation.

But Woodford is not alone in lurching dramatically outside of his circle. Fellow high-profile UK fund manager, Anthony Bolton, who enjoyed tremendous success managing the Fidelity UK Special Situations fund between 1979 and 2007, came out of retirement in 2010 to begin investing in the domestic Chinese A-Share stock market. He came to describe this new investment experience as akin to "looking for gold in a minefield" and lamented the poor standard of corporate governance in China.[5]

He stepped away from managing his China fund in 2014, commenting: "I was wrong about the market as a whole. I thought it would go up over four years. It is down over four years."

As much as we may criticize these overconfident fund managers for believing that their circle of competence is far wider than it is, we are all complicit. The reverence that managers enjoy fuels their hubris and we support their follies by giving them more of our money.

We also only want to deal with simple, binary questions, so we think someone is either a good or bad investor. And if they are defined as good, we are happy to support them turning their hand to anything in the incredibly broad sphere of investing.

There is nobody to prevent their excursions into uncharted waters.

Where are the checks and balances?

It is important that we do not rely on the companies that star fund managers work for. The star managers usually wield too much power.

Companies cannot afford to lose the revenues that star managers generate, so they are hugely incentivised to indulge them. They also know that anything attached to their prized manager will be saleable to the public. Individuals working in risk and compliance have little hope of exerting any control – they are likely to be relatively junior and considered expendable. If they go into battle against a star fund manager, there is only one winner.

In the case of Woodford, he ran his own company, so if someone working in the risk department wanted to raise concerns about the exposure to unquoted companies, they would be doing so to their own boss.

Not a great career move!

If a fund manager is a star, is it too late to invest?

It may appear ironic that in a chapter cautioning against investing in star fund managers I have liberally quoted the two most famous investors of their generation in Warren Buffett and Charlie Munger. Does this mean they are the exception to the rule? No. While I would strongly advise anyone with an interest in investment to read all the Berkshire Hathaway letters to shareholders and anything Charlie Munger has written or said about mental models or investor psychology, I wouldn't invest with them now. Not because of hubris or circle of competence, but the sheer size of assets they are responsible for, allied to their increasing and inevitable delegation of investment responsibilities.

Any of the problems I have mentioned in this chapter should be enough to dissuade us from investing with star fund managers.

Of course, at any point in time there will always be a group of fund managers whose track records and reputations appear unimpeachable. Telling satisfied investors that it is a bad idea to invest with these managers is a fool's errand. The performance numbers don't lie.

Investing with star fund managers always feels comfortable until it doesn't. We simply have to look at the unprecedented (and easily forgotten) fanfare Neil Woodford received after he launched his own venture.

Not every star fund manager will have such a catastrophic downfall as Woodford. Some will fade with a prolonged whimper. The rare exception might even bow out on top. But the arithmetic is not on their side and the probabilities are not on ours. If a fund manager is already a star, we are too late.

The focus of this chapter has been on the dangers of investing with the celebrities of the asset management industry, but isn't the problem far wider than that? The average performance of all active funds is poor, so shouldn't we be avoiding all active managers rather than just the stars? Well, it is not quite that simple, and we will find out why in the next chapter.

Ten-point fund investor checklist – star fund managers

1. **What specifically is the fund manager good at?**

   If we want to have ongoing confidence in a fund manager, we must know exactly what their skill is so we can be sure that they stay within their circle of competence. Outperformance is not a skill.

2. **How has the amount of assets run by the manager changed through time?**

   Both within the fund and in other mandates. Rising fund assets narrow the opportunity set of a fund manager. Higher assets reduce future returns and increase risk.

3. **In what areas of the market has the manager been successful?**

   We must know where a manager has added value in the past to judge whether they can repeat this in the future. If they have made all of their money in smaller companies this may no longer be feasible if the fund size is too large.

4. **Does the manager hold large ownership stakes in certain companies?**

   A red flag for potential liquidity problems is large ownership stakes of companies.

5. **How has the liquidity profile of the fund evolved?**

   Growing assets under management almost inevitably leads to increased liquidity risk. A fund manager's ability to quickly raise cash is likely to be compromised.

6. **Is the manager making frequent, high-profile media appearances?**

   A key warning sign of increased hubris and star status is a fund manager's willingness to have a media presence, often discussing subjects well outside their circle of competence.

7. **Is the asset management business reliant on the manager?**

   How much power and influence is the manager likely to hold?

The more dependent on an individual manager a business is, the less likely that business is to place appropriate controls and restrictions around them.

8. **Has the manager altered their investment approach or started to invest in new areas?**

Star fund managers often operate outside of their circle of competence either because of ego, or the size of assets managed being so large they have to do something different.

9. **How strong is the past performance of the fund?**

The stronger the past performance, the more we should worry about the prospects for future returns.

10. **Has the business taken steps to limit the capacity of a fund?**

A critical signal for incentive misalignment issues is where an asset management company fails to staunch or stem flows into a star fund manager. They know that the fund will be impeded by persistently large inflows, but the profit motive is overwhelming.

CHAPTER 2

THE DEATH OF ACTIVE FUNDS HAS BEEN (SOMEWHAT) EXAGGERATED

THIS CHAPTER WILL change the way you think about the rise of index funds.

I have been working in the fund industry since 2004. Without any doubt the defining feature of my career has been the growth of index fund investing. Not only are index funds cheap, but for years their returns have trounced their floundering active rivals.

Improved performance and lower fees are an irresistible combination. Why would a fund investor do anything but invest in index funds?

The answer to this question is not quite as straightforward as many people now believe. This chapter shows why.

I demonstrate that the success of any active strategy is less about the fund and more about the market environment, while dispelling the myth that the US is the most efficient equity market and close to impossible to outperform. I then describe some simple decision-making rules that will help investors who want to own active funds.

I have managed multi-billion-pound portfolios investing solely in index funds and believe that they are an essential option for all fund investors. I begin this chapter, however, by showing that, far from being the only way to invest, the classic index fund approach can sometimes be the worst.

Are index funds always the best choice?

The war between active and index fund investing appears to be over. Low-cost, market-tracking index funds have vanquished their more expensive and complex rivals. In the ten years to the end of 2020, only 25% of active funds managed to deliver outperformance.[1]

The index fund industry has also enjoyed astonishing growth, rising from less than 5% of equity fund assets in 1995 to 48% by 2020.[2] There is no sign that this dramatic reshaping of the asset management landscape will cease anytime soon.

For many investors, this movement has been a validation of the seminal work of Charles Ellis and William Sharpe. All the way back in 1975, Ellis argued that active management was a "loser's game" where the rise of sophisticated institutions had removed any hope of investors consistently making money by picking stocks. Later, in 1991, William Sharpe presented the elegant case that if active funds in aggregate made up the market, then their average return after fees must be worse than it.

Underperformance was an inevitability.

It seems so simple: there is no other way to invest but into an index fund. Performance has been strong for years and the evidence is overwhelming. Investing in active funds is nothing more than wilful and costly ignorance.

Not so fast.

In 2013, researchers at City University, London released a pair of papers reviewing the effectiveness of market capitalisation weighted stock market indices (the methodology employed in most index funds) and compared it with other approaches.[3]

Given the success of index fund investing in recent years, we might think you could guess the results of the study. But we would be wrong.

The study found that between 1968 and 2011, the best investment decision was to do anything but allocate by market cap weights. And I mean anything.

A market cap index is one where the weights of the companies are dictated by their value (number of shares multiplied by the share price). The bigger the company, the more prominent it is in the index. Most major stock markets indices are constructed in this way (S&P 500, MSCI World, FTSE All-Share). It represents the aggregate views of all investors, and it has become the simple, default investment option. It is also the benchmark against which all active funds are judged. When I refer to index fund investing in this chapter, I mean a market cap weighting approach. Anything else can be considered active.

Improved performance was produced by creating millions of randomly generated portfolios – the proverbial monkeys throwing darts at *The Wall Street Journal*. In a latter paper, even picking stocks based on the Scrabble score of the company's stock ticker beat the market.

It is worth reiterating – selecting and weighting stocks by any means was better than the traditional index fund approach.

This is a puzzling outcome. On the one hand, it is becoming received wisdom that it is foolish to do anything but invest in index funds; yet there is compelling research that for a prolonged period it was the worst possible method to adopt.

So, which is it?

We will explore and answer this question through the chapter. To begin, we need to go fishing.

How likely is it that an active fund will outperform an index fund?

Imagine there are two fishermen, let's call them James and Tom. We are asked to guess which one will catch the most fish in one hour.

James is a skilful fisherman with years of experience, while Tom has been fishing for less than a year and only knows the basics.

This feels like an easy decision for us to make.

We are then given some further information. James's advantage in skill and experience means that he is expected to catch 50% of available fish in the hour, whereas Tom is projected to land only 10%.

Our choice gets easier still.

James is objectively and clearly the better fisherman, and we are being asked to judge who will catch the most fish. Surely, we can now confidently select James?

If we do, then we are making a choice without being aware of the most important piece of information. We don't know how many fish there are to catch.

James is talented, but unfortunate; his lake is barren and few fish pass through:

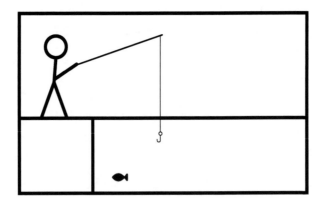

Despite possessing significant skill, James's odds of success are low because he doesn't have the opportunity to catch many fish.

Tom has little ability but is lucky. He is fishing in a lake abundant with fish.

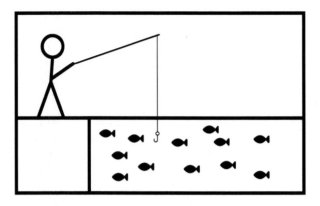

There are so many fish, he doesn't need to be that skilful.

In the hour, ten fish pass James and he catches 50% of them. A haul of five fish. There were 100 fish in Tom's area and he lands 10%, catching ten fish in total.

As Tom wins the challenge, it would be easy to assume that he was more skilful than James, despite his abilities being significantly inferior. Yet the outcome had little to do with individual talent – it was just that the odds were heavily on Tom's side.

Why does a simple fishing analogy matter for fund investors? Because the success of active funds relative to index funds is all about how many fish there are to catch. And this changes through time.

This is exactly the situation faced by active funds operating in the US equity market. For a significant period of time there just haven't been many fish to catch.

Why is the US equity market a graveyard for active funds?

One of the most common utterances of fund investors in recent years is about how difficult it is to outperform the US market. So difficult, in fact, that we should not even try. The argument runs that because it is the most prominent and forensically analysed global stock market, it is far tougher to identify companies that are mispriced. In investment jargon it is referred to as an highly 'efficient' market.

The data – at least in more recent times – seems to support this notion. In the decade to the end of 2021, active funds in the US were trounced by index funds. Only 17% managed to outperform the S&P 500.[4]

If the US is a particular problem for active funds, then there must be some other markets that are more attractive. One frequent example is the UK. Here, the success rate for active funds over the same period was much higher – 38%.[5]

But why was there such a discrepancy?

The common claim about market efficiency doesn't seem to hold water. Although the US market is significantly larger, both the UK and the US are researched by scores of analysts and investors. We might expect niche or frontier markets to have investment opportunities arising because of a lack of sophisticated investor participation, but the UK, like the US, is home to one of the world's largest stock markets.

If not efficiency, then what?

The answer is the environment. Over the ten-year period there were just many more fish to catch for active managers in the UK than the US.

The composition of the US and UK stock markets is strikingly different. We can see this simply by observing the largest ten companies by market capitalisation in the US and UK stock markets as at the end of 2021:

	US	UK
1	Apple	AstraZeneca
2	Microsoft	Shell
3	Alphabet	BHP
4	Amazon	Unilever
5	Tesla	Diageo
6	Meta	HSBC
7	Nvidia	Rio Tinto
8	Berkshire Hathaway	GSK
9	United Health Group	BP
10	JP Morgan	British American Tobacco

From the start of 2010 the US market came to be defined by a group of immensely successful technology and consumer-related names, while the UK's largest firms included pharmaceutical, commodity and banking stocks.

The disparity between the two markets could hardly be starker. One was defined by growing, successful firms that were deemed part of a new economy, whereas the other was led by troubled, old economy businesses.

But why should this be a problem for active funds? Surely, the composition of the market should not impinge on their ability to add value? Unfortunately, it does. For two reasons:

1. First, active funds have a strong tendency to invest in smaller companies. It is rare to see them overweight the largest companies in a market. Indeed, investors in an active fund may recoil at significant exposures to such names. *Why am I paying additional fees to buy Amazon, Microsoft and Apple?*

2. Second, and most importantly, when the biggest companies dominate market returns it reduces the odds of success. It means that a smaller group of stocks has outperformed the market, so an active fund's chance of finding them is greatly reduced. There are only a few big fish to catch, rather than a shoal.

How can we tell whether it has been a difficult or easy environment for active funds? There is a useful tool we can use to observe how challenging it has been to outperform: the equally weighted index.

An equally weighted index – as the name suggests – is where all constituents have the same percentage weighting irrespective of the size of the company. In the US, Apple with a market cap near $2.5trn has the same exposure as Costco with a size of $200bn. In a market cap weighted index the weighting would differ by 10x; in an equally weighted structure it is the same. For the S&P 500, with 500 constituents, all company weightings will start at 0.2% (0.2% x 500 = 100%).

The performance of a market cap weighted index will be heavily biased towards the fortunes of the largest companies. This cannot happen in an equally weighted structure, where all stocks have the same influence.

If a market cap index is producing better returns than its equally weighted counterpart, this tell us that the largest companies in the market are outperforming and the opportunity set for active funds is lean.

If an equally weighted index outperforms, it means any stock selected at random is likely to produce higher returns than the market cap index. An ideal scenario for active funds and dart-throwing monkeys.

Between 2010 and 2020 there was a sharp contrast in the environment for active managers in the UK and the US.

In the UK, larger companies lagged and the equal weighted index produced significantly higher returns than the market cap index.

The 'average stock' outperformed the UK market

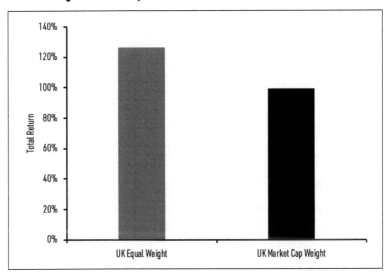

There was no such disparity in the US, where the market cap index produced a return marginally greater than its equally weighted counterpart.

The 'average stock' underperformed the US market

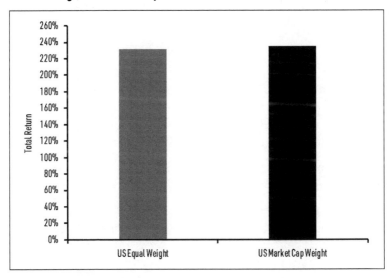

Over this period, it was just far easier to be a successful active manager in the UK than in the US. A random selection of stocks should, on average, have beaten the UK market.

It had nothing to do with efficiency.

If stock market returns are dominated by a select group of the largest companies, most active funds will underperform, irrespective of whether they have investment skill, because the odds are against them. There are just not many fish to catch.

When the largest companies in the market struggle, lots of smaller companies outperform and active funds prosper. It doesn't matter about skill. Anyone can catch a fish.

The US is not significantly more efficient than a market like the UK. Nor is the UK fundamentally a better place for active funds. It is simply that market conditions and structure have conspired to make it appear so over recent years.

While the US has been a bleak market for active funds, a protracted period of underperformance by the largest companies would see the proportion of managers outperforming rise significantly. This would likely lead to headlines about how US active funds have "improved" when it is just a shift in the cycle.

This takes us back to the beginning of this chapter.

The jarring contrast between the success of index fund investing in recent years and its struggles between 1968 and 2011 can be explained by an evolving market backdrop. We moved from a world where being invested in the largest companies was a drag on performance, to one where it became the only effective investment strategy.

The investment landscape changed, which meant the odds of success for active funds deteriorated dramatically.

Given that the chances of us finding an outperforming active fund are so dependent on the prevailing environment, it should be the first thing that fund investors consider. But it is not. In fact, it is often ignored. This is a glaring omission.

If we can better understand the odds of success, we might even be able to better judge when we should invest in active funds.

When should we invest in an active fund?

Fund investors do not ignore the critical question of how difficult it is to outperform an index fund; we just look at the wrong information. The typical approach is to consider only data such as the SPIVA Scorecard, which shows how many active funds underperformed their benchmark over different time periods.

The problem with such metrics is that they are devoid of context. They do not tell us anything about the opportunity set faced by active funds during this period, and therefore it is impossible to judge whether it is a permanent feature, or simply a cyclical phenomenon.

It is this approach that has led to the consensus view that the US market is the most difficult to outperform for active funds. As I have shown, it has certainly been an horrendous period for active US funds, but has this always been the case?

In a word, no.

In the ten calendar years from 2000 onwards, the average return on active large cap US funds was better than S&P 500 index fund returns on nine occasions.[6]

This is puzzling. Did the US market lurch from being inefficient and easy to outperform, to being ruthlessly efficient and impossible to beat in the space of a decade?

The answer is, again, no.

So, what did happen?

The key point to note is the year that the spell of active fund outperformance began – 2000. This was the end of the dot-com bubble. In the years prior to this, the US equity market was engulfed by mania surrounding internet-related companies. Technology (or quasi-technology) companies enjoyed stratospheric returns and overwhelmed the market. By the close of 1999, six of the largest ten companies (by market capitalisation) were technology-related names – including Microsoft, Cisco, America Online and (the little remembered) Lucent Technologies.

As we have already learned, concentrated markets led by a narrow range of large companies make it incredibly difficult for active funds to outperform index funds. But the reverse is also true. The painful unwinding of the dot-com craze meant that those same companies that led the market to the stratosphere were now dragging it back down to earth. As most of the companies in the market were not internet related (as much as they might have claimed to be during the bubble), the majority would go on to outperform the overall market. Life became a lot easier for active funds.

Using the equally weighted index as a tool

The relative fortunes of an equally weighted approach compared to market capitalisation waxes and wanes through time. We can see this by observing the rolling five-year returns of the S&P 500 market cap weighted index against the equally weighted version.

S&P 500 market cap weighted versus S&P 500 equal weighted – rolling five-year returns

The chart shows the stark impact of the late 1990s internet mania for active investors. The ascendancy of a narrow subset of the index enjoying almost unprecedented momentum meant that the market cap weighted index routed its equally weighted cousin. To beat an index fund in this period, active fund managers had to invest in a small group of stocks, at increasingly eye-watering valuations.

It is not surprising that very few active funds prospered through these years.

The dramatic demise of this technology-driven bubble in 2000 brought about a remarkable reversal in the market backdrop. The same select group of companies that led the market to unsustainable highs were now suffering catastrophic losses.

This was a particularly painful scenario for the market cap weighted index, which had inevitably come to be dominated by the names in the eye of the storm. It went on to endure a prolonged run of severe underperformance against the equally weighted index.

For active funds, which had suffered the most exacting period possible through the late 1990s, the backdrop could not have become more conducive. The demise of large, internet-related companies meant that anything that wasn't in that category was probably outperforming the market cap weighted index. All that was required to beat it was to avoid or hold less of the darlings of the dot-com bubble. The opportunity set had transformed from desolate to resplendent.

The contrasting fortunes of active funds in the US through this period had little to do with skill or efficiency; it was about market structure and environment. The odds of success for active funds are cyclical. They vary through time. Sometimes it is hard, other times simple.

A dot-com bubble redux?

The environment in the early 2020s certainly had echoes of the late 1990s. Active funds had been trounced by simple market cap, index funds as a narrow group of large technology-related companies – the technology/consumer giants (Meta, Amazon, Apple, Microsoft and Alphabet) – led the market for many years.

There are differences, however. As we can see from the previous performance chart, the outperformance of the market cap weighted index against an equally weighted index has been meaningful, but nowhere near as pronounced as in the late 1990s. Also, the current group of market-leading, technology-orientated firms are far more profitable (in general) and robust than many of the speculative names from the earlier period (they actually make profits, for a start).

Despite these distinctions, it would be naïve to ignore the concentration of the US equity market. The largest five companies in the S&P 500 (Apple, Amazon, Alphabet, Microsoft and Meta) came to account for more than 20% of the market cap weighted index, a greater level of concentration than at the peak of the dot-com bubble.

From here, the fortunes of active funds relative to index funds will be heavily dependent on the success of these companies. If they continue to prosper then the trends of the 2010s will persist and the rise of index fund investing will continue unabated. If they struggle, then the current fervour for index funds might just cool.

Make no mistake; being solely exposed to index funds is assuming that the trends of recent years will continue and the dominance of the largest companies will persist unabated. Far from being a neutral position, this is a strong investment view and one that is not supported by the full body of evidence.

It is sensible for even the more ardent index fund advocate to consider whether some exposure to active funds would be prudent. There is no reason to believe that there are some ingrained features of a market cap weighted approach that make it superior to others. It is almost certain that there will be periods in the future when it performs worse than many other strategies.

The more concentrated an index becomes in certain stocks and the more an equal weighted approach underperforms, the greater the potential cost of doing nothing but holding index funds is likely to be. This is what history tells us.

Investors who have the appetitie for holding active funds, and can manage the behavioural challenges that come with owning them, can potentially improve outcomes and be better diversified.

But how should an investor who wants to use active funds go about it?

How much should we invest in active funds?

If we were told that over the next ten years, 100% of active funds would underperform a simple index fund approach, how much would we invest in active funds?

The answer should be nothing.

What if we were told that over the next ten years, 100% of active funds would outperform a simple index fund approach, how much would we invest in active funds?

The answer must surely be everything.

This simple thought experiment provides us with our framework for understanding how much we should be investing in active strategies.

Our allocation split between active funds and index funds should be equal to the probability of active funds outperforming.

But how do we know what the probability is?

Our starting point should be 50%. There are two reasons for this:

1. A market cap weighted index fund represents the aggregate views of all investors (ignoring fees for the moment), therefore we should expect half of all active funds to outperform it and half to underperform it. This is a simplification, but a useful rule of thumb.

2. The relative performance of a market cap weighted index fund and other approaches varies through time. If we cannot confidently predict which will be superior, then a 50% allocation is an appropriate neutral view.

This 50% weight works, all other things being equal – but as we have learned through this chapter, other things are not necessarily equal. There are environments that are likely to favour active funds and environments that are likely to prove far more challenging. There is no way we can precisely predict this, but we can use the equally weighted index as a useful guide.

If we witness a period where we see unusually strong performance from index funds compared to equal weighted, it might be prudent to increase our allocation towards active funds, as it is likely that their opportunity set will be more attractive in the future. If we see the opposite and index funds are underperforming, then we should do the reverse and increase our exposure to index funds.

We can think of it as a rubber band being stretched. The more one approach outperforms the other, the more likely the prospect for a significant reversal of fortunes.

How do we do this in practice?

It is important to reiterate that nobody should try to aggressively time exposure between index funds and more active strategies – that is a fool's errand. Our default should be to do nothing. We should only consider adjusting if there is evidence of extreme dislocations. Our approach could be as follows:

1. Judge whether we have any appetite to invest in active funds.

2. Start with a 50/50 allocation between pure index funds and preferred active approaches.

3. Ensure any allocation to active funds is appropriately balanced and diversified. Don't put 50% in index funds and 50% in a 20-stock high conviction growth fund.

4. Remember that active just means different from a market cap index fund approach – low-cost active funds should be our starting point.

5. Rebalance annually back to a 50/50 split between active and index funds.

6. Only alter the target 50/50 weight if two thresholds are met:

   • The performance of an equally weighted index relative to market cap index is historically extreme. In most mainstream equity markets a 20% differential over five years would be a reasonable threshold. This information is available from MSCI and major data providers such as Lipper and Morningstar.

   • A valuation gap is evident between equally weighted and market cap indicies. If one is historically cheap or expensive relative to the other, it may suggest an opportunity to improve future returns. We can look at metrics such as price to earnings ratios or price to cash flow to assess this. A disparity of at least 20% should be the minimum.

7. If we have a scenario where either equally weighted or market cap weighted has materially underperformed and is significantly cheaper than its counterpart, it may prove prudent to modestly adjust our base 50/50 weighting.

8. We may want to further shift our weighting as the performance and valuation becomes more extreme. We should, however, set a limit. A 50/50 default with a 60/40 maximum tilt would be sufficient for most investors.

There are two important points about this approach.

First, it is not a timing tool. As we saw in the late 1990s technology bubble, the performance and valuation disconnect between equal weighted and market cap can become incredibly extreme. There is no accurate way of gauging how far things will run or when they will change.

Second, this is not an approach for everyone. Moving away from a 50/50 split is for those with the risk appetite to attempt to get the odds on their side as the opportunity set changes. It is perfectly reasonable to stick to rebalancing back to 50/50 and nothing else.

What about fees?

The obvious riposte to allocating 50% or more to active funds is that after their higher fees are considered, far more than half will underperform index funds. This only holds if we adopt a very narrow and traditional view of active fund management. It is no longer about lavishly paid fund managers on Wall Street attempting to pick stocks. Anything that is not an index fund approach can be considered active. We can now be active without incurring high costs.

There are a multitude of options available to fund investors to gain broad market exposure in a way that deviates from the index fund default. It is possible to invest directly into funds tracking equally weighted indices. There are smart beta or alternative index funds that adjust the naïve market cap weighted approach and bias stock weights towards companies that are cheaper, more profitable, or less risky.

There are also funds that mirror indices weighted by corporate fundamentals, where rather than being based on market capitalisation, the size of a company in the index is based on crucial factors such as sales or earnings. Unfortunately, there is no current option to invest in stocks based on their Scrabble scores.

There is a broad range of active funds that adopt a different weighting approach from a traditional index fund but don't come at a materially higher cost. If we have another period like that between 1968 and 2011, where a market cap weighting approach becomes the worst possible option, these types of funds will likely find favour.

Are index fund investors prepared for a different environment?

The timing of the City University study that I began this chapter with was unfortunate, as it coincided with a dramatic upswing in the performance of a market cap weighted investment approach. The study argued that everything outperformed a market cap weighting methodology and for years after nothing did. It was a complete reversal of the findings of the study. It now looks as if the study was deeply flawed.

But it wasn't, it was right.

In the time covered by the research there were significant periods of outperformance by market cap weighting; it was just that over the full period covered its returns were poor relative to other approaches.

The study tells us two crucial things:

1. The relative performance of index funds compared to active approaches will be highly cyclical and vary considerably over time. There will be prolonged spells when one looks vastly superior to the other (before fees).

2. Ignoring fee considerations, there is no reason to believe that the market cap, index fund approach should consistently outperform other approaches.

Unfortunately, most of us have forgotten these two vital pieces of information. As investors our time horizons are frighteningly short, and we care only about evidence that is recent and available. A decade or more of strong results from index funds and poor results from any active fund is all the evidence we need. Many investors have never seen anything but stellar results from index funds, so why would we believe anything else?

Conflated arguments

At its heart the case for index funds has been built upon two arguments that have been incorrectly conflated. First, that controlling fees is critical to long-term investment success. Second, that a market cap weighted approach to index fund investment will consistently lead to superior returns over time. The contention on fees is incontrovertibly true; the argument about market cap weighting is not. It is just that performance over recent years makes it look like it is.

The inexorable rise in index funds has transformed the asset management industry and has been an overwhelming positive for the investing public. All investors should hold exposure to index funds. As with any investment trend, however, there is a danger that the narrative supporting it is taken to unjustifiable extremes.

It is perfectly reasonable for investors to be allocated entirely to index funds. That is likely to prove a sensible route to solid long-term outcomes. It is dangerous to assume, however, that there is something innate in a pure market cap weighting approach (outside of fees) that makes it an inherently superior, unimpeachable way to invest.

It is hard to imagine now, but it is almost certain that we will have years and decades in the future when the environment returns to the one observed in the City University study – where an equal weighted methodology outperforms a market cap weighted index and the odds of success in using alternative approaches improve markedly. Fish will again become abundant.

Although there will be environments that are more conducive to investing away from index funds, there are certain types of active strategies of which we should always be exceptionally wary. In the next chapter I will examine one such example – funds that exhibit smooth performance – where investors are lured in by the prospect of serene returns and are blind to the true underlying risks.

Ten-point fund investor checklist – when to invest in active funds

1. **Are index funds a viable option in the asset class?**

    In some areas, index funds are sub-optimal or simply not feasible. The trading costs in high-yield bonds make market-tracking approaches unpalatable, whereas in private equity there are no investable indices to track.

2. **What are the biases of the chosen index?**

    Investing in an index fund is not a neutral choice. The selection of a particular index will have embedded investment views, such as whether it contains smaller companies.

3. **What is the structure of the market?**

    How concentrated is it in a select group of companies? The more skewed towards a particular set of companies an index or market is, the more variable the success of active management will be.

4. **Is the market biased towards certain types of stocks/companies?**

    Markets can become horribly biased towards certain in-vogue areas, such as technology in the late 1990s. This creates short-term performance pain for active funds, but paves the way for future opportunities.

5. **What proportion of active funds have been successful in the market/asset class historically?**

    Data such as that provided by SPIVA is useful for ascertaining the historic performance of active funds versus index funds.

6. **Why have active funds fared well/poorly?**

    It is not sufficient to know how successful active funds have been in a particular market; we need to understand why. Only then can we take a view on whether patterns are likely to persist.

7. **How has a market cap weighted index performed relative to an equally weighted index?**

    The more extreme the outperformance of a market cap weighted index against an equally weighted index, the more difficult the environment has been for active funds, and the greater the chance of some reversion. Performance data is available via MSCI and providers such as Lipper and Morningstar.

8. **How does the valuation of a market cap weighted index compare to an equally weighted index?**

   Valuation also matters. The more extreme the valuation of a market cap weighted index against an equally weighted index (on measures such as a price to earnings ratio), the better the prospects for active funds in the future. Valuation data is available via MSCI and providers such as Factset and Bloomberg.

9. **What is an appropriate fee budget?**

   Managing the cost of fund choices is critical to long-term returns. Setting a cap on costs will limit the impact of negative compounding.

10. **Are low-cost active/alternative index funds available?**

    There should no longer be a distinction between high-cost active funds and low-cost index funds. It should be possible to access funds that take an active approach at a low cost (such as smart beta or alternative index funds).

CHAPTER 3

SMOOTH FUND PERFORMANCE CONCEALS RISK

E XPERIENCING SEVERE SWINGS in the value of our funds is one
of the toughest parts of being an investor. Even if our investment
horizons stretch far out into the future, the pain of short-term losses
can be acute and lead us to make terrible decisions.

One way to avoid such problems is to invest in funds that rarely suffer
from price fluctuations.

There are certain types of fund with performance that seems to be
persistently on a tranquil, unperturbed, upwards trajectory. While
our other holdings are buffeted by changing market and economic
conditions, these funds appear impervious.

The lure of anxiety-free fund investing can be irresistible, and its
appeal is understandable. Yet it is so often a bad idea.

In this chapter I explore why funds offering an apparent panacea of
high returns with little risk are worth avoiding, and how widely used
risk metrics such as volatility and correlation have been misused to sell
funds with smooth performance in popular areas such as private equity.

Although there are many hidden risks within funds exhibiting smooth
performance, there is also an undoubted behavioural benefit to their

stability. I detail a simple behavioural trick that can replicate this advantage with any fund.

But I begin with a classic example of smooth returns masking severe underlying problems: so-called death bonds.

Why did anyone invest in death bonds?

I recall early in my career being handed a factsheet for a fund by a colleague. At first, I thought it was a cash fund, because the line on the performance chart moved from bottom left to top right in a linear fashion at something close to a 30-degree angle. On closer inspection I realised that it could not be cash, because the returns were far too high. The name of the fund was not familiar, so I assumed it was a hedge fund, but in fact it was even more esoteric. It was a strategy investing in life insurance policies, often called traded life policy investments (TLPIs).

The approach of the fund was to buy policies from individuals living in the US with impaired life expectancy. The individual on whose life the policy was insured would receive a lump sum payment. The fund would continue to pay the premiums, before receiving a payout on the death of the insured.

This was certainly not a mainstream asset class, and I knew next to nothing about the details or complexities of investing in this area. What was particularly puzzling was how positive my colleague was about prospects for the fund, given that their level of knowledge was similar to my own. The curiously attractive risk and return profile was overwhelming all other considerations.

Finding the Holy Grail of investing

My colleague was not alone. This type of strategy became popular in the retail market in the UK, with one fund raising assets of more than £600m. Given how they were marketed, it is not difficult to see why. It was quite literally framed as a "Holy Grail" investment product.

The below quote is taken from a marketing piece for a TLPI fund that appeared in a UK investment publication:

> Investors are always looking for the Holy Grail of absolute returns – low volatility, low risk and decent net returns of 8–10% through open-ended funds with monthly dealing, in an asset class that has no correlation to other investment markets. Add a socially responsible element, and you have an ideal investment.[1]

The fund had it all: high returns, low risk and little relationship with other more traditional asset classes. It even managed to squeeze in a spectacularly dubious social responsibility angle. With characteristics like that, why invest in anything else?

When outcomes are good everything else is ignored

One of the simplest and most effective investment rules is: if the returns look too good to be true, don't invest.

When the outcomes delivered by a fund are inconsistent with reasonable expectations, this should serve as a warning – not a justification.

The presentation of unrealistic and unsustainable returns does not necessarily point towards wrongdoing (though this may be the case). It could just be that there are underlying risks within the fund that are hidden. Or that it has simply enjoyed a fortuitous run of unusually strong performance.

Whatever the case, we should avoid it.

Unfortunately, this rule of avoidance is very rarely followed. Quite the contrary. We are often drawn into investment funds because of the appeal of smooth returns.

This was certainly the case for TLPI funds marketed to UK investors. Here is the long-term performance of a prominent fund sold into the UK market:

TLPIs – smooth sailing and then choppy waters

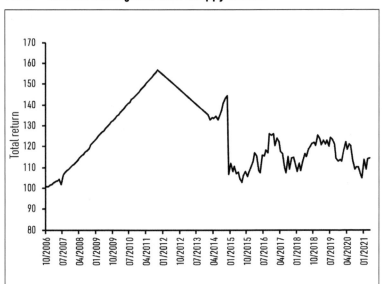

Until 2011 it did look like the Holy Grail of investing. Annualised returns were close to 9%, while volatility and losses were almost entirely absent. Those who had enjoyed these returns were not aware or worried about the risks that lurked beneath the surface. They were singularly focused on the performance being delivered.

Even when problems began to emerge in the asset class, people retained faith. The below comment is from an investor in a TLPI fund in response to an article which stated the UK financial services regulator was considering a ban of "ponzi-like death bonds":

> I've seen a steady 8% per annum return on my investment EVERY year. This is the only asset class of investment that has delivered consistent results in recent years.[2]

As disaster loomed on the horizon for the retail-orientated TLPI funds, investors were willing to laud historic returns and the performance profile.

Smooth and high returns from a fund always mean that there is an underlying complexity that most of us cannot hope to fully understand. Absent a true awareness of how a fund generates returns, we will lean evermore heavily on what returns a fund has produced. This leaves us incredibly vulnerable to poor decisions.

A toxic ending

The death knell for TLPIs as a retail product in the UK came in 2011, when the UK financial services regulator (now the FCA) branded them "high risk" and "toxic" and began a consultation on banning their sale to retail investors.[3]

Among a catalogue of potential risks, the regulator highlighted poor liquidity, the challenges around valuation methodology and mortality assumptions, and the complex web of parties typically involved in TLPIs as primary concerns.[4] If risk is viewed as only price volatility, none of these threats were readily apparent when observing the performance of the funds.

The regulator was correct. These were higher risk offerings. The smooth performance allowed them to masquerade as low risk funds. TLPIs were inappropriate for all but the most sophisticated investors. Unfortunately, while the regulator's pronouncements were valid, they caused a surge of outflows from TLPI funds in the UK. As scrutiny on the risks of these funds increased, panicked investors inevitably rushed for the exit.

Unlike stocks and shares – where investors can trade freely with each other at any given moment – there is no such marketplace for TLPIs. This left many funds unable to raise the required cash to meet redemptions, and they were forced to suspend dealing.

Investors were trapped.

The years that followed brought a litany of fund closures and valuation write-downs. Investors suffered an arduous wait to see any of their capital returned.[5] A group of disgruntled investors even took the UK regulator to court, claiming that the intervention had breached their human rights.

The focus on the debacle of TLPIs being sold to retail investors in the UK is often on the activity of the regulator, the features of the asset class and the dubious behaviour of some operators in this space.

While these are all valid issues, the overarching lesson is about the perils of funds with smooth performance.

The problem is not only that those smooth returns serve to mask risks and complexity within a fund; it is that they are transformed into a marketing tool. It plays on our aversion to losses and uncertainty.

Smooth performance is extolled as a feature when it is a bug, leading us into ill-judged investment decisions.

What causes a fund to have smooth performance?

For all but the safest investments, smooth performance from a fund is typically evidence of poor liquidity – meaning the underlying assets are very difficult to buy or sell. Unlike stocks (primarily traded on an exchange) or even most corporate bonds (primarily traded directly between counterparties, rather than on an exchange), the securities in a fund with smooth performance are unlikely to be easily traded.

Limited liquidity has significant ramifications for investors looking to access their money, but it also impacts how a fund is valued. Absent a healthy secondary market where prices can be set by investor demand and supply (so-called marked to market), securities held in funds with smooth performance are likely to be marked to model. This means that the price of each underlying security is derived from an opaque financial model, not what other investors are willing to pay for it.

The second-by-second fluctuations we see in global stock markets are all about investor psychology – the ebb and flow of fear and greed. They have very little to do with genuine changes in the value of the cash flows that a company might produce.[6] When security prices are marked to model, this human behaviour – the central driver of short-term performance fluctuations – becomes an irrelevance. Prices are instead set by obscure and arbitrary models, on an infrequent basis (often monthly or quarterly), which leads to an unusually stable performance trajectory. In the case of TLPIs the valuation model was heavily influenced by actuarial assumptions about life expectancy, amid a host of other inputs.

Although an absence of price variability is appealing, there is an array of problems. Foremost is the fact that the valuation of the fund will often not reflect a realistic tradeable price for the securities it holds. When we look at the valuation of a fund we own, it is reasonable for us to expect that we can trade at close to that price. If a fund is marked to model, the value ascribed is based on the underlying assumptions used; little thought is given to the price we could realise if we wished to sell today.

A valuation of $100 is meaningless if, when we attempt to sell, the price available in the market is only $50.

Smooth fund performance is the result of a fully functioning secondary market not existing for a set of securities, where there is no trading of sufficient magnitude or frequency to create a viable price. This is unequivocally a drawback and material risk for investors to consider. Yet it has been transformed into an advantage, a means of increasing the saleability of a fund.

How is such a distortion possible, and why are we so susceptible to it?

Is volatility a good measure of the risk in a fund?

Investment risk is a fiendishly difficult concept to define. Not only is it multi-faceted – the prospectus for a range of simple index funds lists 26 different risk factors – but its meaning will depend on the circumstances and objectives of each investor. To simplify this complexity, the asset management industry uses volatility as shorthand for risk. Volatility is the variability of the price of a security or fund. Funds with smooth performance exhibit very low levels of volatility.

How much the price of a fund fluctuates is an incredibly important risk factor and investors should care about it, but volatility is only one form of risk; it is not risk itself.

Using risk and volatility as interchangeable terms can be deeply misleading when it comes to funds with smooth performance. This is vividly apparent in the following chart, which displays the price performance of a mutual fund and an investment trust, both investing in commercial properties.

Smooth property versus marked to market property

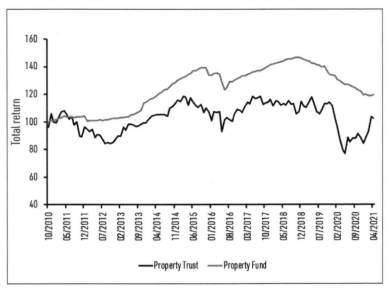

The underlying assets held are remarkably similar, but the price volatility is significantly different. Why? The valuation methodology.

The more volatile price of the trust is based on investor supply and demand (marked to market), while the fund's valuation is based on the appraisal of property valuers (marked to model). This creates the anomalous situation where similar assets are valued in an entirely different fashion. This can become particularly problematic during periods of severe market stress when mark to model strategies exhibit stale pricing because they are slow to reflect new market or economic conditions.

If we view risk solely through the lens of volatility, then a marked to model approach becomes incredibly attractive, particularly for asset managers looking to sell products based on high returns and low risk.

Volatility as a target (applying Goodhart's law)

This widespread adoption of volatility as the pre-eminent measure of risk for all funds has created an environment where the metric itself is often misused and has become less meaningful. This is a situation known as Goodhart's law. Formulated by economist Charles Goodhart, the law states that when a measure is utilised as a target it ceases to function as an effective measure. This is because when individuals understand the end objective, they will do anything to achieve that target – irrespective of how they get there.

The classic story demonstrating this behaviour is one of hardware factories in the Soviet Union. When a target was given to workers based on the number of nails produced, scores of miniscule, useless nails were made; when the target was instead based on weight, giant useless nails were created. Although this is likely an apocryphal tale, the perils of Goodhart's Law are frequently in evidence.

In 2020, as Covid-19 swept through the UK, the government pledged to carry out 100,000 tests per day by the end of April. This herculean task seemed unachievable until the last moment. On the final day of April, 40,000 tests were posted out in the mail and counted in overall testing numbers even though many of the tests were never used.[7] The government hit the target, but their method of reaching it rendered it meaningless.

When a target is set we can quickly lose sight of the reason it was set in the first place. The target for many investment funds has become risk-adjusted returns – with volatility the measure of risk.

How are smooth performance funds used to flatter outcomes?

The notion of risk-adjusted returns is a theoretically sensible one. It says that we should judge the quality of the results delivered by a fund not only by its returns but also by the risk it has taken to deliver them. It is better to have a 20% return while taking little risk than a 20% return where we risk everything.

The problem lies in our use of volatility as the measure of risk and the behaviours it encourages.

Earlier in my career I worked at an asset management company and ran a portfolio that invested in a range of different funds. I was competing against many other fund managers doing similar things. The main method of comparison and assessment was the risk-adjusted returns we produced. Clients wanted to know how I was doing against my peers. Should they stick with me or go somewhere else?

The target for all the funds in this area was superior risk-adjusted returns. To meet this objective the fund managers could try to enhance their performance, but that was easier said than done. There was a far simpler and more certain way to improve risk-adjusted returns: reduce risk by bringing volatility down.

An easy way to do this would have been to add a fund from an asset class with lower volatility, which would be particularly effective if it also had a low correlation with the rest of the holdings in the portfolio. For example, adding a government bond fund to a portfolio dominated by equity funds will reduce risk because they have a very low or negative correlation to equities (when stock markets fall, government bonds are typically stable or rise) and experience lower volatility.

Correlation in this context is a measure of diversification; it can range between +1 and −1. A low correlation simply means that there may be a weak relationship between two variables. If two funds have a performance correlation of +1 then they have moved in the same direction at the same time. If they have a correlation of 0 then the performance of one fund has been entirely independent from another. If you add a fund to a portfolio, and the new fund has the same volatility as other holdings but with a low correlation, the expected volatility of the overall portfolio will reduce.

There is, however, a major drawback with this approach.

Investing in a lower risk asset class should reduce returns. Although bringing down volatility, adding government bonds to an equity portfolio would also mean sacrificing long-term returns.

What fund managers really needed were funds that had a similar return potential to the other holdings in their portfolios but appeared to have significantly lower risk.

Funds with smooth performance were the perfect option.

To improve risk-adjusted returns, fund managers didn't need to find funds where the underlying securities were distinct to what they already owned, just those that exhibited smooth performance because the securities they held were not marked to market.

It did not matter if the smooth performance funds were investing in the same underlying assets that were already held in the portfolio. Marked to model pricing meant it would appear as if they were differentiated simply because they were priced and valued in a different way.

As if by magic, buying funds with smooth performance can maintain a portfolio's return potential while reducing risk.

It is easy to see why the use of volatility as the standard risk metric in the asset management industry is wholly inappropriate for funds with smooth performance, but rather than leading us to avoid them it has encouraged their use. All investors assessed on their risk-adjusted returns (with volatility as the measure of risk) are incentivised to buy funds with smooth performance.

There has been no bigger beneficiary of this than private equity.

How risky is private equity?

Alongside the rise of passive, index fund investing, one of the key trends in recent decades has been the increasing willingness of investors to move from traditional equity markets to private equity, investing in companies that are not publicly traded on a stock market. The major recipients of this shift have been buyout funds, which take over established companies, and venture capital funds, which invest in fledgling businesses.

The move towards private equity was led by the prominent US endowments in the 1980s, but its use has since become more widespread, although public markets still dominate – global assets in private equity reached $6.3trn in 2021.[8] In 2017 fresh capital raised from private markets outstripped public markets for the first time.[9]

There has been a range of factors driving investor allocations increasingly towards private markets. Part of this is simply a desire to ape the behaviour of the large and sophisticated US endowments. This move has been boosted by general disillusionment with the performance of other non-traditional strategies, particularly hedge funds.

Asset managers have also played their part in extolling the virtues of private assets. As they continue to suffer outflows because of the shift from active to index fund investing, lucrative private markets offer them a route to protect their margins in an asset class that cannot be effectively replicated in a low-cost index fund.

Outweighing all these contributory reasons for the shift is the purported performance of private equity strategies, which often appear to offer higher returns and lower risk than public markets.

Unfortunately, both the return and risk measures commonly used are illusory.

Much of the scrutiny in this area has been on the questionable and unsustainable returns quoted by many private equity funds.[10] Yet it is not simply the often-unobtainable returns that lure investors in, it is the path they take. Private equity is another asset class that enjoys the benefits of mark to model pricing and the resultant smooth performance profile. It is often sold as an asset class which offers material diversification benefits when held alongside standard equity funds investing in stock market listed securities.

This is a puzzling claim.

A typical private equity buyout fund will be comprised mainly of small and medium-sized companies, often with a healthy dose of leverage applied.[11] How can this have a low correlation with public market equities? Are the companies owned by private equity funds exposed to a different economic cycle? Are they immune to recessions?

Of course they are not.

The diversification comes from the mark to model valuation and the resultant smooth performance profile.

In an investment world obsessed with volatility and correlation, private equity appears to be an asset with great diversification benefits. Mark to model pricing means that private equity funds do not experience many of the sharp drawdowns seen in public markets. Leading wealth managers frequently extol the diversification provided by the illiquidity and valuation methodology of private equity:

> Private equity can help reduce portfolio volatility, diversify return streams with an asset class with low correlation to public markets, and potentially improve returns.[12]

The trouble with viewing private equity as a diversifying asset which offers drawdown protection is that it can lead to a misunderstanding of the genuine risks involved. The smooth performance and diversification benefits may be apparent in most market conditions; but when a crunching economic downturn arrives these features will evaporate. The losses will likely be as severe (if not worse) than public markets; they might just arrive a little later – when the models catch up with the reality.

The most dangerous form of diversification is the one that vanishes when you most need it.

The idea that a fund investing in private equity is materially different from one exposed to public equities is nothing more than a sleight of hand facilitated by smooth performance.

Performance will be smooth, until it isn't.

How can we make our funds have smooth performance?

One of the most persuasive marketing features of funds with poor liquidity such as private equity is the concept of an "illiquidity premium". This is the notion that there should be an additional reward for owning an asset class where it is difficult or costly to access our money. There is no skill required to realise it; it is simply compensation required by an investor for the lack of flexibility and choice we will have.

Although there are studies seeking to ascertain the existence of an illiquidity premium, their focus is on the wrong thing. Any benefit that might stem from owning assets that are difficult to trade is not structural, it is behavioural. The perceived drawbacks of such funds are actually an advantage.

Most of the behavioural problems that plague investors are a combination of our reaction to the fluctuations in the price of an asset and our ability to freely trade it. Funds with smooth performance and poor liquidity largely remove the stresses of performance variability that tempt us into injudicious decisions. Even if we want to trade, in many cases we cannot.

Illiquid funds with smooth performance inadvertently promote long-term investing.

This is not a reason to invest in this sort of fund, as the behavioural advantages may be outweighed by other risks. Crucially, there is a simple behavioural trick that replicates the features of funds with smooth performance.

Check fund performance less frequently

Our susceptibility to short-term decision making is driven by how we engage with the funds that we own. Resisting the often overwhelming temptation to obsessively monitor our investments and trade too frequently is extraordinarily difficult. Trading in funds has become seamless, but to encourage long-term thinking we need to replicate some of the unintentionally positive features of smooth performance funds.

The easiest way to do this is to stop checking the valuations of the funds we own. If we only looked at the value of our funds less often, we would experience less performance variability. This would not make us immune to losses, but would reduce the constant emotional and behavioural strains of reacting to daily swings in price.

If we had only been checking our funds on an annual basis, we would have entirely missed the savage and swift share price falls seen in early 2020 as global markets were gripped by fears around the economic ramifications of Covid-19.

The next chart shows the price performance of the S&P 500 based on two different observation periods – every day and every year – between 2016 and 2021.

S&P 500 daily and yearly price performance 2016–2021

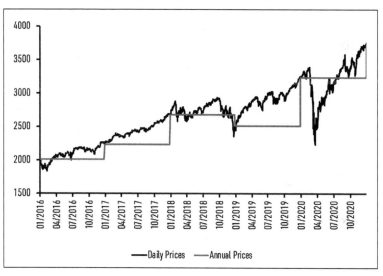

As the period between observations is increased, the return becomes smoother and the experience of gut-wrenching price changes greatly reduced. In the first quarter of 2020, the S&P 500 endured a peak to trough decline of 34% and lost 12% in a single day but recovered to post an 18% gain over the entire year.

To enjoy the profit, we had to live through the stress and anxiety of the losses. For many the temptation to sell during such periods can be overwhelming.

The best protection is to smooth the performance of our funds by checking them less frequently. Not only does this encourage a long-term approach, it is far less behaviourally taxing. We won't react to difficult spells of performance if we don't feel them.

If we believe that we must keep a constant eye on performance for fear of what might occur, then we are probably invested in the wrong funds.

Checking our funds less regularly is not the only nudge we can apply to mimic the attractive features of smooth performance. Another critical behavioural intervention is to limit our ability to trade by adding a little friction.

The benefits of friction

We can artificially smooth performance by changing the frequency of our observations, but that does not stop us trading, which most funds allow us to do daily. One effective method for reducing unwanted behaviours is introducing some form of friction. Making small steps to make something harder to do can have a dramatic impact on even profound decisions.

In the UK it is estimated that limiting the amount of paracetamol tablets in one packet led to a 43% decrease in the number of deaths by overdose. The intervention seems immaterial to the scale of the decision, but small amounts of friction really can change behaviours.[13]

This concept can be used to slow our investment decision making. On a personal level we might let a friend or family member have the password to our brokerage account; on a professional one we might insert an additional layer of sign-off before a trade is approved. Neither step recreates the stringent liquidity restrictions that can be a feature of funds with smooth performance, but adding a little friction can go a long way.

Should we ever invest in a fund with smooth performance?

To suggest we should never invest in a fund with smooth performance is wrong. Rather we should never invest in a fund *because* it has smooth performance. At best smooth performance means that the underlying assets are illiquid and often valued at prices that are detached from reality; at worst it means severe opacity and perhaps malfeasance. We must also avoid spurious claims about diversification and correlation that are caused purely by the valuation methodology, as opposed to economics.

We can, however, learn lessons from these funds. We find them attractive because they allow us to worry less about short-term volatility and often force us to stay invested for the long term. The challenge for us is to capture these features, while avoiding the dangers that can come with funds reporting smooth performance.

Aside from masking risk, smooth performance can also obscure the complexity inherent in how a fund makes money. Investing in something we don't understand is always a bad idea and, in the next chapter, I will explore why investors should favour the simple option.

Ten-point fund investor checklist – smooth performance funds

1. **Why does a fund have smooth performance?**

   Smooth performance is telling us something about the underlying securities in a fund.

2. **How are the securities in the fund valued?**

   Smooth performance is typically the result of the securities held within a fund being priced by a model rather than the market.

3. **Who is valuing the securities in the fund?**

   It is not simply how the prices for securities in a fund are being derived that is important, but who is doing it.

4. **How liquid are the underlying securities in the fund?**

   Marked to model pricing means that there is unlikely to be a market from which a reasonable price can be taken. No viable market will mean poor liquidity.

5. **Does the liquidity of the securities match the liquidity of the fund?**

   The major liquidity risks in funds typically arise when there is a mismatch between the liquidity offered by a fund and the liquidity of the securities it holds. A daily dealing fund holding infrequently traded securities is a recipe for problems.

6. **What are the primary risks in the fund not captured by its volatility?**

   Volatility is a woefully inadequate measure of risk for a fund with smooth performance. It is dangerous to assume smooth returns means low risk; it is often quite the contrary.

7. **What are the diversification benefits of the fund?**

   Funds with smooth performance are often used because of their diversifying characteristics – they behave differently from other funds. Yet this is often simply because they are priced differently, not because the underlying securities are genuinely distinct.

8. **What is the primary rationale for investing in private equity funds?**

    Smooth performance is not sufficient justification to invest in private equity as this is simply a function of the poor liquidity/ lack of tradeable market. There must be other reasons to make a strong case to invest.

9. **Would we own the fund without smooth performance?**

    We should only own a fund with smooth performance if we would still own it without the smoothed results.

10. **How frequently do we check the performance of our funds?**

    The more regularly we check our funds, the more volatility we will experience.

CHAPTER 4

CHOOSE SIMPLE OVER COMPLEX

FINANCIAL MARKETS ARE awash with complex investment funds. These allow asset managers to charge high fees because of the supposed sophistication on offer, while investors are enticed by irresistible promises of strong returns through all market conditions.

Promises that are so often broken.

In a fiercely competitive environment with growing pressure on fees and profitability, complexity has become a solution for the asset management industry – but it is a problem for fund investors.

In this chapter I explore how we can define complexity in a fund and why it is so dangerous. I also unpack why we are happy to invest in funds when we have no idea what we are buying. Finally, I argue that while the golden age of returns from simple investment funds is over, this is no time to be drawn back towards complexity.

But first I look at an investment strategy known as XIV and how complexity can quickly turn sour.

What is the attraction of a fund that is guaranteed to fail?

The product was known as XIV. It bore all the hallmarks of a classic complex investment. It was a strategy that only professionals could begin to understand but was accessible to retail investors. It enjoyed a period of astonishing performance. It raised $2bn in assets. And then it blew up.

XIV was an exchange traded note issued by Credit Suisse. It was one of several exchange traded products engaged in a practice known as volatility selling. It is almost impossible to explain what this means in simple terms – always a good test for complexity – but I will try.

The XIV strategy was based on the VIX index – the so-called Wall Street 'Fear Gauge'. The VIX index utilises the price of options (to buy or sell in the future) on the S&P 500 to measure investor expectations around share price fluctuations. The more volatile markets are expected to be, the more value there is in holding an option.

If investors are worried, and they expect more share price volatility, the VIX will rise. If investors are sanguine, less variation is expected and the VIX will fall.

It is used as a measure of investor uncertainty.

The VIX evolved from being a gauge to a product when futures contracts were launched based on the index in 2004. These allowed investors to trade around their expectations of volatility. If we were worried about a market crash we could buy VIX futures, which would rise in value as share prices fell and volatility spiked.

XIV took the other side of this trade. It was exposed to short VIX futures, so benefited when market conditions were calm, but suffered during periods of stress. Think of it like selling a disaster insurance policy. We happily receive a steady premium for years but lose everything when the hurricane hits.

The structure of XIV meant that at some point it was almost certain to end badly. Even the prospectus of the note said the long-term expected return was zero. A severe spike in volatility on any given day would lead to a forced liquidation and investors seeing their holding all but wiped out.

Investing while the Sword of Damocles hangs over our heads is never a good idea, so why did so many people invest in XIV?

Perhaps it was held by sophisticated investors who used it in a prudent and deliberate fashion. Perhaps not. XIV had its own Reddit user group, and after its demise Fidelity banned retail investors from using such short-volatility products (a little too late).[1] A lawsuit was even launched against Credit Suisse by disgruntled holders.[2] Hardly the behaviour of professional investors who understood the risks they were taking on.

So why did investors buy such a dangerous strategy?

We can strive tirelessly to understand the reasons why people buy a particular investment product, but it is usually a needless exercise. The answer is almost always performance. There will be other motivating factors, other explanations will be given, but strong past performance is the necessary and sufficient condition for making most investments. The story of XIV is no different.

From its launch in 2010 until its dramatic demise in 2018, XIV had enjoyed the tailwind of not only a prolonged bull market in equities but one which was notably tranquil. Between 2010 and its peak in 2018 XIV produced an incredible return of 1,350% compared to "just" 171% for the S&P 500.

Much of this stratospheric performance was delivered across 2016 and 2017, with 2017 one of the least volatile years in market history. Volatility was declining, equities were subdued, investors were complacent. It was the perfect environment for XIV to deliver strong performance and attract new investor flows. Across those two years it returned 421%.

The calm was laying the foundations for the storm.

XIV versus S&P 500 (returns XIV launch to peak)

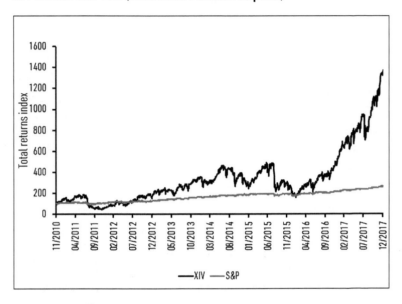

The end of XIV

The downfall of XIV was as swift as it was inevitable. Investment strategies are always vulnerable to a reversal of fortunes following a spell of stellar performance. XIV took this pattern to the extreme. The results delivered across 2016 and 2017 that so enticed investors, directly increased the risk of disaster. By 2017 the VIX had fallen to such a historically low value that a swift move even towards only average levels of expected volatility threatened to wipe out XIV.

VIX index history

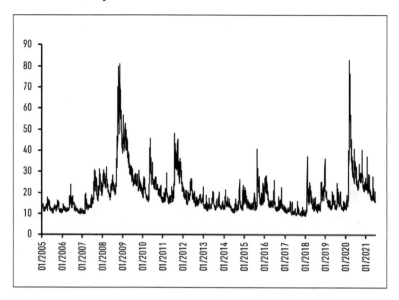

The structure of the note meant that if the VIX index rose sharply on a single day an acceleration event would be triggered. This meant that the fund would be wound up before it lost more than 100% of its value. This happened on 5 February 2018.

Although the S&P 500's decline of 4% on this day was unremarkable by historical standards, it was a shock to market participants after months of equanimity. Fear had returned. The VIX index exploded by 116% – the highest single day move on record – as investors rushed for the exit. The insurance had been called in and XIV investors were about to foot the bill.

XIV launch to liquidation

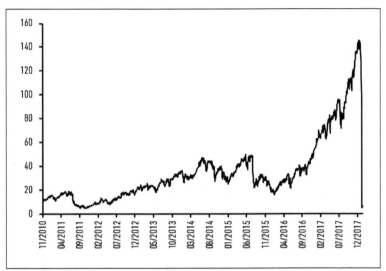

The case of XIV is the perfect example of the problems of complex investment strategies. XIV was impossibly complex and wildly unsuitable for all but the most knowledgeable investors. It was also designed to fail.

If we do not understand how returns are being produced, then we cannot hope to comprehend the risks we are taking.

What is a complex investment fund?

There is a straightforward test for judging the complexity of an investment fund. Can we explain how it makes money to a ten-year-old?

For equities, I can easily describe owning a portion of Amazon and being entitled to a share of its profits. Even though bonds are more challenging, the concept of lending money to Apple and receiving a regular interest payment should be intuitive enough.

Now try a forward start interest rate swap.

But it is not just about the use of individual, esoteric instruments. A feature of complex funds is that they are often impossible to simplify in any reasonable manner. Can we define the essence of what they are trying to achieve? While one position or trade might be comprehensible, once they are combined with others all we are left with is an impenetrable web of investments.

This brings us to another essential test for a complex investment fund: looking at a list of holdings. The more indecipherable it appears, the more complex it will be and the more caution we should exercise.

A complex investment fund is almost always a black box. We might know the inputs (such as seeing the holdings) and we can observe performance, but we can never truly see the pieces in the middle. Just a jumble of component parts with little clarity as to how or why they fit together.

Investing in complex funds is not about our analytical capabilities; it is often an article of faith. We do not know how a complex fund makes money. We have no meaningful evidence. Only belief.

When is complexity a good thing?

In our everyday life we are constantly engaging with complex items, objects and issues. Showing faith in things that we don't fully understand. We don't just accept complexity; we actively embrace it because it makes our lives better in a multitude of ways.

Why is it that we use complexity to our material advantage in many parts of our lives, but should avoid it when investing?

If I take a flight from London to New York or undergo a heart bypass operation, then I am taking on the risk of complexity to provide some benefit to myself. Although I know the basics of how a plane flies, I couldn't build one. And while the surgeon might explain the procedure to me, I wouldn't fancy my chances of performing the operation. Much like investing in a complex fund, in these situations I am unaware of the full detail of what is occurring and am beholden to the expertise of others.

But unlike the complex fund, this opacity is acceptable.

Complexity can be acceptable and even superior to simple options but only when it meets certain criteria:

No viable alternative that is as good

It is only worthwhile to take on the risk that comes with complexity if it provides a materially better outcome. This is obviously the case in my flight from London to New York (a cruise ship might take a week), but not so in the case of complex alternative investment funds. For many years, such funds have trailed the performance of simpler strategies.[3] Additional complexity risk for lower returns. Not particularly appealing.

Consistently applied approach

We can be more confident in complexity where it is consistently and comprehensively applied. In other words, do lots of people do it? Although not homogenous, all major passenger planes are broadly similar in how they function. The complexities of one 737 are largely analogous to another's. Conversely, all complex investment funds are distinct and heterogeneous. While we cannot fully understand these funds, we do know that each one will have its own idiosyncratic risks. Not only that, but the risks in each fund will change over time. The behaviour of an individual fund in the past or the behaviour of complex funds in aggregate tells us extraordinarily little about the specific risks that one fund may carry right now.

Tested and proven

We should only be comfortable with complexity if it is tested and proven. This is usually in the form of widespread adoption. The 40 million commercial flights that take place each year not only provide a test for the robustness of the planes but allow us to have some understanding of the types of risk we take on when flying. If the number of aviation disasters increased tenfold, our understanding of the complexities of flight would not alter, but our willingness to take the risk of this type of travel likely would.

Specific expertise

Although not a failsafe, acceptable complexity is usually deployed by those with appropriate and evident expertise. We understand that the surgeon carrying out our operation has undergone years of training to hone the specific skills required for the task. This gives us comfort that we don't need to comprehend the intricacies of their job. It is impossible to gain a similar level of confidence around the supposed expertise which is used to manage and sell complex investment funds. The only evidence of expertise will come from past performance. By virtue of it being a complex fund we won't really know how that performance has been delivered.

We also don't know whether the historic results are down to luck. Whenever results can be materially influenced by chance, judging expertise is difficult. Even if previously strong results were a consequence of skill, there is no reason to believe that the future will be as conducive. A stable environment is crucial if we are to be comfortable with complexity.

Risk and costs are known

Complexity is also acceptable where we can be confident that the risks and costs are clear. Using a dishwasher is a more complex option than cleaning the dishes by hand, but there is a reasonable upside and limited risk (although the ultra-cautious may decide that the risk of a house fire is too great).

Purpose is clear

Understanding the purpose of complexity can also be incredibly useful in identifying whether it is a deliberate ploy to mislead or befuddle. Always ask – does it need to be this difficult? The reams and reams of unfathomable legalese used in terms and conditions on websites are designed to prevent us from grasping something, usually because the company in question wants our personal data. Virtually every investment fund fraud uses complexity as a shroud to cloak the nefarious activities being undertaken.

Costs of rejecting complexity are high

We may reasonably take on complexity risk if the cost of not doing so is pronounced. If we had an illness that gave us three months to live, pioneering treatment would fail some of the previous tests but still be an attractive option given the known cost of declining.

On occasion the opportunity costs for complex investment funds will be high, as there will always be certain funds that produce exceptional returns, but on average there is little or no cost to avoiding them. Furthermore, the risks involved can be severe; both from blow-ups and disasters, or years of disappointing returns and high fees.

We shouldn't pour scorn on complexity; it brings us a vast array of benefits and is often a consequence of brilliance and rare expertise. Our lives would be a great deal poorer if we avoided everything that we did not understand completely. Yet it is dangerous to assume that more complexity means better outcomes. Complexity is only attractive where it is proven to be advantageous and the additional risks can be reasonably understood.

Why do we buy complex funds, and why do asset managers sell them?

Embracing complexity improves our lives but can also come with significant costs. The challenge is differentiating between its useful and dangerous guises. Our default setting is to assume that the more complex something is, the better it is at achieving its goal. This is an understandable but problematic heuristic.

If we have two competing options and one is more complex, we are likely to believe that the complex option had more energy expended in developing it – *why would they go to the trouble if it wasn't an improvement?* And, as we probably won't understand the complex choice, we are likely to give a great deal of credit to those who thought of it – *I have no idea how this works; the people behind it must be pretty smart.* Complexity is also likely to come at a higher price, further buttressing the idea that it is a sign of quality and progress.

As with most heuristics, they are not without merit and are rational in many situations. As things evolve, they often become more complex. From the abacus to the electronic calculator; the horse drawn carriage to the motor car. Technological developments that make things quicker, easier and more efficient almost always come from specialist expertise – based on ideas and principles that most people cannot hope to understand. As a society we have become accepting of complexity as a feature of progress. We don't want or need to understand how. Just give us the results.

In addition to wanting the benefits provided by complexity, we also like what it says about us. This is particularly true when it comes to complex investment funds. If we invest in something complex, then it is a signal that we understand it. While everybody else is investing in pedestrian equity and bond funds, we have the intelligence and sophistication to do something different.

We don't just buy complex funds because we believe they might give us better outcomes; we buy them because they make us look better. The asset management industry is a more than willing seller.

Why does the asset management industry sell complex funds?

Simplicity is a problem for the asset management industry. If an investment fund is transparent, simple and replicable then it can be copied by almost anyone, and the main means of competition is through ever lower prices or capricious performance. The prolonged and dramatic shift towards index funds from actively managed funds has been disastrous for most asset managers who have seen severe outflows and declining margins. To stop this haemorrhaging of assets and fading profitability, it is imperative that they can offer something different – something that cannot be readily copied and for which they can charge higher fees.

Complexity is the answer.

A major contradiction exists at the heart of complex investment funds. Investors often don't need them, but asset managers must sell them. The more complex or unfathomable an investment fund, the better it is for the asset manager. Strategies that rely on the inexplicable brilliance or skill of an individual, team or system are perfect. They are like a patent or a bespoke product. We can only get them *here*.

The sales pitch for complex funds is straightforward:

- We have a product that can produce returns that are both better and different than what you currently invest in.

- You can only get it from us.

- You won't be able to understand it (if you could everyone would be doing it).

- We are very clever (we understand it).

Complexity has become a requirement for asset management firms. While some will thrive in the world of simplicity – through scale, brand, distribution or good fortune – most will continue to struggle. When we are being sold a complex fund, it is imperative that we understand the inherent incentive problem that exists. We need to think of complexity in investment less as sophistication and advancement, and more as a business imperative. And a dangerous one at that.

Does complexity increase fund risk?

We might consider complexity to be little more than a glossy sales pitch trying to tempt investors into paying high fees by presenting lofty and unachievable aspirations, but that would be ignoring a central problem of complex funds. While they are often sold based on the notion that they reduce risk compared to more conventional investments – purporting low drawdowns and low correlations – their very complexity can imbue them with far greater risks than their simpler counterparts.

Complexity in investment is not a risk mitigant, it is an additional risk.

In 1984, sociologist Norman Perrow published a book entitled *Normal Accidents*, which explored the idea that failure and disaster are built into certain systems by virtue of their complexity.[4] His primary example was the partial meltdown at the Three Mile Island nuclear power station in 1979, where a blocked water filter precipitated a chain of events that resulted in a near disaster. In such instances the risk stems not from a major and obvious technological failing, nor a glaring human error, but the ripple effect of a minor issue in a complex, deeply interwoven system.

Perrow's theory identifies two features of complex systems which render them particularly vulnerable: how many moving parts there are and how reliant the parts are on each other. If there are numerous dependent elements in a system, then one minor fracture can have disastrous consequences.

Perrow's ideas matter a great deal for our understanding of complex investment funds. Almost all use an array of different strategies and trades, then amplify their exposures by applying a liberal dose of leverage. The use of leverage to boost returns is often justified by the idea that all the positions in the fund are doing different things. When one trade zigs, the other zags. At face value, this reduces the risk of a fund because the complementary trades offset each other.

But problems arise when these relationships falter. Financial markets change quickly and relationships break.

If every position in a fund starts behaving in the same way, a supposedly low risk portfolio built of many independent parts becomes high risk and – in Perrow's words – tightly coupled. The leverage can quickly turn this ripple into a tsunami.

One of the most famous complex fund blow-ups in history – Long-Term Capital Management – was a direct result of the problem of leverage meeting a breakdown in correlations. The fund was designed to generate high returns without undue risk by applying leverage to small pricing anomalies in related securities (such as off- and on-the-run treasuries). After enjoying stratospheric returns in its early years, it collapsed in spectacular fashion in 1998 when market conditions altered dramatically following Russia's decision to default on its debt.

As stated in a report on the incident by the President's Working Group on Financial Markets: "The simultaneous shocks to many markets confounded expectations of relatively low correlations between market prices and revealed that global trading portfolios like LTCM's were less well diversified than assumed."[5]

Incidents like that suffered by LTCM show how complex investment funds can meet Perrow's criteria of a normal accident. Naïve assumptions made by superficially rigorous risk models about independence, low correlation and low risk can be torn asunder by relatively small changes in the environment. The impact of this is magnified by the leverage applied. Funds such as LTCM are designed to fail. They just need a spark.

Complexity does not solve complexity

Not all complex funds are LTCM and most will not suffer a similar fate. Many, however, carry risks that are far greater than we can see from their history or risk models.

One of the major weaknesses of such funds is that they attempt to solve a complex problem with a complex solution. Complexity is sold as a necessity to both exploit markets and protect us from them. It seems that because financial markets are unimaginably intricate and convoluted, we feel that complexity is the best way to deal with them.

This is exactly the wrong approach.

Adding complexity to complexity compounds risk rather than quells it. It exposes investors to unknown and unintended consequences. There is an arrogance around complex investment funds, an underlying notion that those involved can somehow tame the perplexing nature of markets with intelligence and sophistication. Yet in the battle between complex financial markets and complex investment funds there is only one winner.

Complex funds require us to believe in magic

Arthur C. Clarke's statement that "any sufficiently advanced technology is indistinguishable from magic" could easily be applied to complex investment funds. Like magic, their workings are both extraordinary and unexplainable.

As investors, how can we possibly make informed decisions about funds that we cannot understand? We might be able to make a relative judgement between complex funds – fund A is preferable to fund B because it is more transparent, carries less leverage and is more liquid – but that is all. We are rarely in possession of enough evidence to make an informed absolute choice.

Of course, we can never have full confidence in even the simplest investment. We don't know what will happen tomorrow. Our global equity market index fund might lose 40% in a crunching recession next year. Yet with simple funds we at least have clarity over why they should make money and the types of risks involved. With complex funds we are just left waiting for the rabbit to be pulled from the hat, and so often it isn't.

Is the golden age of simple funds over?

Investing in complexity has been a terrible trade for a long time. A study of institutional investors showed that in the decade from 2008 there was a cost of 36bps for every 10% allocation made to alternative investment strategies.[6] When so-called smart money institutional investors sought to prove their moniker by investing in more elaborate funds, they ended up reducing their returns.

All that work and toil. They would have been better off keeping it simple.

There is, however, a caveat. Have investments in alternative strategies really been so bad, or has it just been that simple solutions have enjoyed a prolonged and unsustainable period in the sun? A combination of strong equity markets and a monumental shift lower in bond yields led to handsome returns for just owning a basic combination of equities and bonds.

Let us take the default simple investment portfolio – 60% global equities/40% global bonds – as an example. Since the early 1990s its average annual return has been close to 8%, and over 365 rolling 1-year periods it has only produced negative returns 17% of the time.

The most basic (and cheapest) investment option has delivered for decades, not only producing high returns but with very few periods of painful drawdown. Doing anything but sticking with this option has likely been a bad idea.

But things are unlikely to be so rosy in the future. If we make some simple valuation assumptions about equity and bond returns, we can see that at the end of 2021 a reasonable expected return from a global 60% equity / 40% bond portfolio was close to the lowest it has been for 25 years. A combination of derisory bond yields and high equity multiples meant that the expected annual return from this point was close to 2%, compared to a 4% average and over 7% at its peak.

Global 60/40 portfolio expected return

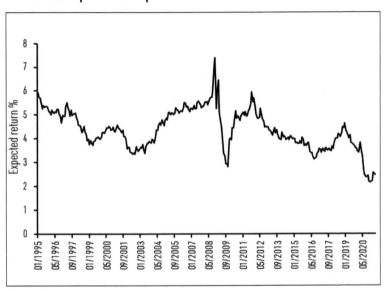

Perhaps complex, alternative strategies appear inferior only when looking in the rear-view mirror, and the future is much brighter because they offer the chance to maintain the higher returns that are no longer available in simple strategies.

Is now the time to embrace complexity and reject simplicity?

In a word: no.

We should not be altering our investment approach. The only thing we should be changing is our expectations. As investors, we need to accept that there will be periods when valuations are expensive and yields are low, and our future returns are likely to be poorer. This is an inevitable feature of financial markets. There will also be opportunities when the reverse is true. What we must not do is react to the prospect of leaner times by taking unnecessary and poorly understood risks.

The attraction of complexity is never stronger than when the expected returns from traditional asset classes and simple funds are low. As investors, it is difficult to accept – particularly if our most recent frame of reference is of far higher returns. We need to do something to keep our returns at that level. Asset managers will seek to exploit this by marketing complex strategies and claiming that their sophistication offers a way out of the drab returns on offer from simple funds. This might be by extracting some "premium" from illiquidity, investing in a niche area, or by having the capability to make returns regardless of market conditions.

All tempting possibilities.

The problem is that lower returns from simple strategies do not change the risks that stem from complexity. The assumption that more complex strategies are unaffected by the overall environment for investment returns is absurd. Most have failed to add value against a backdrop that could hardly have been more favourable for investors; to expect them to undergo a resurgence when things get more difficult seems an heroic assumption.

Accepting lower returns from simple investments is a far better option than taking on the risk of complexity and reaching for an additional return that has so often proved illusory.

What makes adopting a simple approach so difficult?

Simplicity is a great virtue but it requires hard work to achieve it and education to appreciate it. And to make matters worse: complexity sells better.

—Edsger Wybe Dijkstra

Financial markets are messy and difficult. This feels incongruous with using simple investment strategies that seem too easy, even lazy. But we should not be ashamed to embrace simplicity. There will always be the exception – the complex fund that delivers outstanding returns – but to focus on those rare cases would ignore all the catastrophes, failures and let-downs.

Even if investing in complex strategies had worked for investors, it would still be a bad idea. Investing in things we do not understand always is. But the plain truth is that they have not delivered. Absent any compelling evidence that they offer any benefits to investors, complexity is nothing more than a sales tactic upon which businesses, careers and reputations rely. We will all be better off taking the difficult route and choosing the simple option.

At the heart of the marketing of any complex fund is a narrative about why the sophistication on offer can provide better performance. Although such tales can be persuasive, most of our worst investment decisions are the result of a compelling story. We will find out why stories are so dangerous to investors in the next chapter.

Ten-point fund investor checklist – complex funds

1. **How does the fund generate returns?**

    We should only invest in a fund if we can explain – in simple terms – how it makes money.

2. **What securities does the fund hold?**

    A sensible test of complexity is to look at a holdings list. Is it comprehensible?

3. **Why is it superior to simple options?**

    Complexity must be clearly superior to simpler alternatives.

4. **Is the fund tested and proven?**

    Complexity tends to fail under stress. The less a fund has genuinely experienced exacting market conditions, the less comfortable we should be bearing the risks.

5. **Are our return and risk expectations realistic?**

    Complex funds are often bought based on entirely unreasonable expectations, such as high returns, no correlation with equity markets and very low drawdowns. If this is our investment case, we need to reset out expectations. The complex fund that we invest in will not achieve this.

6. **Is it possible to monitor the fund through time?**

    To have ongoing confidence in a fund we must be able to make regular judgements about its activity (not just its performance). We can only do this if we can see behind the curtain and understand it.

7. **Does the fund use leverage?**

    Leverage accentuates risks and can precipitate dramatic losses.

8. **How reliant is the fund on a lack of correlation between positions?**

    Many complex funds are reliant on an assumed lack of correlation between positions. Risk is reduced because positions behave differently to each other. This creates problems when relationships and correlations break.

9. **When would we sell the fund?**

If we don't understand the intricacies of a fund then our sell decisions tend to be entirely beholden to performance, which means we often won't sell until it is too late.

10. **How exposed are we to the fund?**

If we must invest in complex funds, then we should limit our exposure, so our fortunes are not tied to something we do not fully comprehend.

CHAPTER 5

GREAT STORIES MAKE
FOR AWFUL INVESTMENTS

I T IS EASY to think of investing as a scientific discipline based on profits, cash flows and valuations. But it's not, it's about storytelling. Stories underpin every investment decision we make. They allow us to be persuaded, to persuade others and persuade ourselves.

We make investments in funds based on how compelling the story is, often ignoring critical factors such as the price we are paying. This can lead to disastrously bad investments when we are beguiled by a gripping yarn and ignore the evidence.

In this chapter I explore why we find stories an irresistible and essential way of understanding the markets, economies and the world around us. I consider why thematic or "story" funds are so often a poor investment, and show how we can protect ourselves against dangerous stories by better understanding why we are attracted to them. Finally, I explain why good stories result in bad performance.

I begin by looking at how the asset management industry turned a sensible idea into a dangerous investment story.

Why invest in a "bloody ridiculous investment concept"?

In November 2001 Goldman Sachs economist Jim O'Neill released research arguing that the burgeoning economies of Brazil, Russia, India and China should have a seat at the table in global agenda-setting policy forums such as the G7.[1]

His argument was compelling. The growth of these four countries – where 42% of the world's population resided – dramatically outstripped those of the existing G7 members, which were lumbering, developed nations. In one scenario, Goldman Sachs saw the combined weight of these emerging countries as a share of global GDP reach 27% over the course of a decade. These countries were the future powerhouses of global economic growth, and they deserved a voice.

He anointed them the "BRICs", and the moniker stuck.

Although we might question the validity of combining such a disparate group of countries into something of an amorphous collective, O'Neill's case was valid. These countries were going to disrupt the old order of established economies and demanded attention. The research was so influential that since 2009 there has been a formal BRICS Summit, a meeting of the original four countries plus South Africa.

The research was credible and highlighted the potential for a shifting economic landscape, which has undoubtedly been realised since the paper was published. So, what was the problem?

As usual, the problem started when asset management companies got involved.

The BRIC concept represented a delicious investment idea. The narrative was simple and powerful. The economic growth prospects were far stronger, the demographics were attractive and there was an emergent middle class ready to embark on a spending spree. Why would we consider investing in economies like the US, the UK or Europe? They were the past; these emerging markets were the future.

The first BRIC funds were launched in 2006.[2] Why the delay between the coining of the BRIC term and asset managers creating new products based on it? They were waiting for the final piece of the jigsaw – stratospheric returns. A story alone is rarely sufficient to sell a fund; it needs to be supported by stellar past performance. As the chart below shows, the returns of emerging market equities compared to developed markets were particularly strong between 2004 and 2007. The stars had aligned to sell BRIC-themed funds.

Emerging market equities versus developed market equities (1990–2010)

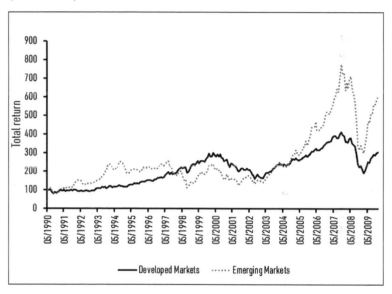

With grim inevitability the performance of BRIC funds from their launch was a disaster, whether compared to broad emerging markets or developed markets. The next chart shows the performance of a BRIC-focused index fund against the broad emerging markets index (MSCI EM) and global developed equity markets (MSCI World).

BRIC fund performance

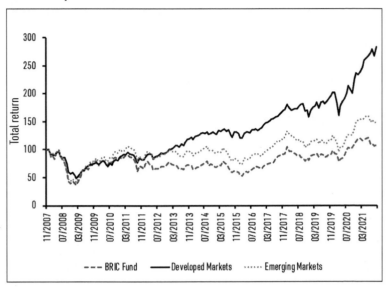

From its launch in 2007 until late in 2021, the BRIC fund returned a paltry 7%. This is not an annualised figure; this is the total return over the entire 14-year spell! Developed market equities gained 183% over the same period. BRICs were a wonderful story and a truly woeful investment.

Looking at the performance history today, it seems obvious that BRICs were a terrible idea. But it is important not to understate the fervour around the concept and the certainty that they would be successful. Hindsight is a wonderful thing. To question the credibility of BRIC funds when they were launched was to be viewed as a luddite.

This is always the case with compelling investment stories. At the peak of narrative fervour and performance, contrary opinions are summarily rejected. When performance turns sour, everyone is incredulous that it could ever have been considered a sensible idea.

As with all powerful investment narratives, the supporting arguments were largely true. These economies had population, prospects and demand. The problem was that by the time this was common knowledge the gains had already been made. If a story is strong enough to launch a fund based on it, it is already in the price.

Investment stories are explanations of the past; we too often treat them as predictions of the future.

The last word on the BRIC fund phenomenon should fall to Albert Edwards, strategist at Société Générale. He presciently labelled BRICs as a "Bloody Ridiculous Investment Concept".[3] It is hard to disagree.

Unfortunately, despite a litany of bad experiences, stories continue to dominate our fund investment decisions.

Is all fund investing about stories?

Humanity is defined by storytelling. It is how we understand the world and how we communicate with each other. Stories can be used for many purposes – to instil values, to educate, to persuade or to entertain – but they are always about explaining cause and effect. Something has happened or will happen, and stories are used to tell us why.

Stories are inherently comforting. Without them we must accept a world dominated by luck and chance, and admit that most things are impossible to explain or predict. This not only plunges us into perpetual ambiguity but undermines our own agency – what about our own stories? Stories are a comfort blanket in an uncertain world.

Given the centrality of stories to human existence, it is no surprise that our investment decision making is driven by storytelling. In financial markets we are constantly seeking to explain what has happened in an economy or a market in the past or predict what will happen in the future. The problem is we can do neither of these things.

Economies and markets are extraordinarily complex; an innumerable, intricate web of interrelated and dependent interactions. It is absurd to believe we can accurately explain what has happened, let alone what will happen. Yet this is what we constantly strive to achieve.

Financial markets are a chaotic concoction of competing explanations. From meaningless descriptions of daily stock price moves to persistently hopeless forecasts about the future, we are obsessed with stories even when we know they are worthless. And why are we obsessed? Because we cannot bear the alternative.

Without stories investors would be left with randomness. Imagine being told that the S&P 500 fell by 2% yesterday due to unexplainable fluctuations. A 2% decline was one of many paths it could have taken. Our brains understand cause and effect; without them we would exist in a financial environment defined by chaos. While this may be closer to the reality, it would not make for a comfortable existence. But although stories can be reassuring, they can also be damaging.

Unacceptable randomness

Nassim Nicholas Taleb coined the term "narrative fallacy" for our inability to see a sequence of data without linking them with a story.[4] We never see a random chain of events, rather a pre-ordained path, with one step inevitably leading to another. Our drive to explain and understand how something occurred means that for every successful company or inspirational CEO there is a backstory to their achievements, a set of circumstances or decisions that led to their triumph. Luck is nowhere to be seen.

The asset management industry feasts on our susceptibility to narrative fallacy. Among the thousands of active fund managers we would expect some to be successful by sheer chance, but asset management firms know that we are suckers for the story. A fund manager's experience, background and temperament will all be presented as part of their inexorable journey to success. Of course they are outperforming.

When we peruse active fund performance tables we are unable to see a set of randomly distributed outcomes; rather we see a set of stories, inevitable failures and richly deserved victories.

If we see the past as an unavoidable sequence of events, then that is how we see the future. Why do we ignore our famed inability to make predictions?[5] Because we look at what has happened in the past and it seems obvious. Hindsight bias is incredibly powerful. The stories we tell about history are so seamless and direct that the future must be equally predictable. When we look backwards, we don't see randomness and noise – we see an arrow.

Telling the stories we want to hear

The stories we create to understand the world are personal. We don't read them, we write them. As Will Storr notes in his book on the science behind storytelling, the types of stories we tell are dependent on our pre-existing ideas, principles and motivations.[6] And much of our storytelling is an effort to defend them. We use stories to persuade ourselves and others that we are correct.

The idea that stories are not simply something that we receive from others but rather create ourselves is incredibly important for investors. When we participate in financial markets we are not coolly and impartially attempting to identify cause and effect; rather we are creating stories that corroborate our positions, views and beliefs, and often rail against those with conflicting perspectives. Stories can be used to justify decisions we are about to make and support those that we have already made.

As investors we tell stories about everything, but we need to be particularly wary of those vivid and powerful narratives that consistently lead us into injudicious decisions. In the fund industry there is a type of strategy that is designed to play on our susceptibility – thematic funds.

Are thematic funds always a bad idea?

A thematic fund is one where the investments it makes are related to a particular theme or subset of a market. Unlike traditional strategies – which are typically broadly defined and categorised by the asset class and region in which they invest – these are founded upon a specific sector, industry or idea. These can be in mainstream areas such as technology and healthcare, or esoteric niches like marijuana and robotics. BRIC funds are a classic case of thematic fund investing.

Despite frequently poor outcomes, thematic funds have enjoyed dramatic growth. By 2021 total assets in thematic strategies had reached $394bn across 662 products.[7] The majority of this came from specialist index fund strategies, reflecting the crucial role that ETFs have played in the increasing prominence of this type of fund investing.

Thematic funds are not going to go away, but perhaps they should.

There is a pattern around the creation of thematic funds. A certain narrow area of the market will generate strong performance. This attracts the attention of investors and the media. These returns will require an explanation, so a narrative develops around why these types of investments have performed so strongly and, crucially, why they will continue to do so. Investor interest is piqued and asset managers spy an opportunity. They then launch concentrated funds tapping directly into this area. These new fund launches both provide a means for investors to access stories directly and serve to stoke the narrative.

Thematic funds are perfect for asset managers as they come with in-built marketing. There is no need to create a story to sell the product; the story is the product. The ease of launching new funds – particularly through ETF structures – means that they can take a scattergun approach. They don't need to pick a single theme, rather they can choose a selection. Some will wither and die, while others will raise assets and continue to outperform for a time. There is no need to worry too much about the investors left experiencing losses or stumbling from one story to the next.

The use of thematic funds speaks to a crucial misunderstanding of the role of stories in financial markets. The standard assumption is that stories create price movements. Investors boost the price of securities because they buy into a particular story. But the causality works both ways. Effect often creates cause. If a fund generates notably strong or weak performance then we need to explain it. Randomness cannot be an answer, so we construct convincing stories to justify the movements. These can be self-reinforcing – a price movement creates a story, the story moves the price, the price move corroborates the story, and so on.

Most thematic funds are price momentum strategies cloaked in a story. There are very few fund launches based on themes that haven't worked well in the years just before they were launched.

Thematic funds are often marketed as seeking to exploit "secular growth", or what we might call structural shifts in economic activity. Yet, ironically, they often feel like fads or flavour of the month funds designed to exploit our vulnerability to a story and for chasing past performance. Investors who think they are investing in long-term change are often being taken for a quick buck.

When we invest in a thematic fund, we are making some herculean assumptions about our own capabilities. We believe we can not only identify long-term economic themes but also find the right fund to exploit this insight and invest at the correct time.

At the time we invest in a thematic fund it feels that everything is right, but we are usually buying at the very worst moment.

In a paper published in 2021, researchers observed the performance of specialist or thematic ETFs after their launch and found that on average they delivered negative risk-adjusted returns. Performance is particularly poor immediately after inception, as these strategies tend to come to market at the point of peak excitement.[8]

This is a bleak but unsurprising set of findings. It is hard to think of a worse time to invest in a fund than when it has produced remarkable returns in the past and is investing in an area that is the focus of everybody's attention already.

Our desire to invest in thematic funds shows how stories are so powerful that they can overwhelm all reasonable evidence; how can investors guard against this?

How do we protect ourselves against dangerous investment stories?

There is a set of characteristics that make investment stories compelling and therefore particularly dangerous. When we can identify some or all of the following seven key elements within a narrative, we need to be on guard against the risks:

1. **Truthfulness**

   It is easy to assume that the most dangerous type of investment story is where we are sold an outright lie, but we are most vulnerable when the story is true. Take the BRIC funds; many of the underlying features of the story were valid. These nations would become a crucial feature of the global economy and generate high levels of economic growth. Unfortunately, the story being true doesn't make it a good investment, just one we are more likely to buy into.

2. **Simplicity**

   Financial markets are far too complex for us to either understand or predict with any confidence; stories relieve that discomfort by simplifying everything. Our brain wants to understand the world. It wants to translate chaos into order. We are drawn to stories that make everything easier. At the peak of BRIC excitement many investment rationales were simplified into – "there are a lot of people in China".

3. **Coherence**

   The structure of stories also matters greatly. If there is a logical order to the story – a beginning, middle and end – then we are more likely to believe it. Academics Reed Hastie and Nancy Pennington tested this idea on jury decisions and found that the ease with which a story could be constructed impacted the perceived credibility of the evidence and the ultimate verdict. It isn't necessarily the weight of the evidence that matters, but whether it flows as a coherent story.[9]

4. **Change**

   Will Storr highlights that one of the most essential ingredients of a gripping story is change. We are wired to detect and attend to it. For investors change means risk and opportunity. The ability to make our fortune or avoid disaster. At the heart of any compelling investment story is a narrative about a change that will have a material impact on prices. The more profound we perceive that change to be, the greater the gains we expect to make.

5. **Salience**

   If a story has our rapt attention, it is likely to influence our behaviour. As an investment narrative becomes more available it feels more important and persuasive. If a story elicits an emotional response, we are likely to take leave of our senses

6. **Past performance**

   Strong past performance is both the catalyst for an investment story to take hold and the evidence used to justify it. Investment stories start and end with performance.

7. **Messenger**

   It is not just the strength of the story that influences us, but who tells it. This is known as the messenger effect.[10] Fund investors are particularly vulnerable to two types of messenger: those with expertise and those with charisma. Expertise is problematic because we are often at an information disadvantage when buying a fund (the seller knows more than we do) and we have no means of fully assessing the credibility of their story. Our inability to effectively validate what they tell us leaves us vulnerable to accepting it based on their status.

   While experts are adept at convincing us a story is true, charismatic individuals make a story lucid and enthralling. Their personality can overwhelm any rational assessment we may wish to make of the evidence. There are few things more dangerous in fund investing than a lucky fund manager with charisma. Great performance and a captivating personality can lead to irresistible stories and painful losses.

Not all these factors have to be in place to make a gripping investment story, but the more that are, the more convincing it is likely to be and the more money it is liable to cost us.

Why do good stories lose money?

There are three reasons why investment stories can prove so costly, and none of them have anything to do with whether the story is right or wrong.

Stories can be too late, too big or too complex.

We invest too late

The most common way that investment stories fail is that we arrive too late. We might also call this "investing when the story is already in the price". Almost by definition, once an investment story takes hold it is already widely known, and the performance of a stock or fund has been strong in the recent past.

If everybody else knows the story, how are we going to make money out of it?

The problem is not simply that everyone else is aware of the theme and so it is reflected in the price, but that the ebullience that can surround a story means that prices could be in fantastical territory. A spellbinding story increases the chances that we are wildly overpaying. We should always assume that everyone else is as violently enthused as we are. The more strongly we believe it, the more enamoured others are likely to be.

It is critical to remember that the validity of the story is largely an irrelevance. A powerful story combined with outlandish performance almost always means hideously expensive valuations. If a fund manager talks about their investments without mentioning the prices they are paying, run for the hills.

Even a great story has its price.

The best protection investors have against the dangers of stories and themes is to simply check the valuation and performance. If returns are unusually strong and valuations stretched compared to the wider market, we should be incredibly wary.

We can make money from stories, even if they are expensive. Trends can persist for years after any reasonable level of valuation is surpassed. But if we do intend to profit from fund investments in this way, it is important to be clear about our approach. We are not investing because of a story; we are investing because of how we think other people are reacting to that story. We might think of this as reflexive or second order investing – not focused on the underlying asset or fund, but the behaviour of other investors. We can generate handsome profits irrespective of valuations in this fashion, provided we know when to get out.

We invest too much

The issue with stories is not simply that they make us prone to buy funds that are likely to turn sour, but they can be so persuasive that they overwhelm our investment behaviour. Our belief in a particular story can be so ardent that we become evangelical about it. We cannot see anything but the one, all-encompassing narrative. This is why the most powerful investment stories tend to end with investors losing not a small portion of their portfolios, but everything.

The stories can be so good that we reach a stage where investing in anything else would seem foolhardy. Diversifying away from it can feel like sacrificing returns. If the scenario does play out as we expect it to then we will regret not investing more.

The risk of over-investing in stories does not have to be a dramatic "all-in" bet; in fact it is more likely to be a slow creep. Our initial investment starts to perform well; it makes more money than anything else we own. We see the performance as justifying the story. We allocate more and more money to it until it dominates our investments. We justify the size of the holding by the strength of the story. But then things change. The story evaporates.

We lose our senses gradually and our money quickly.

If we are investing in a thematic or story-dependent strategy we should assume that it carries very severe downside risk and make it only a small portion of our portfolios. We should never make our financial outcomes dependent on it.

The risks are too complex

Financial markets are inconceivably intricate and complicated. Investment stories disguise this fact. They simplify everything. They make us believe that if X happens Y will follow. It never works like that.

By masking complexity, investment stories lead us to grossly understate the risks that we face. It is hard to imagine a more complicated investment case than the success of the four widely disparate Brazilian, Russian, Indian and Chinese markets. Investors were not worried about this; they were buying a far more straightforward story. They saw the opportunity, not the risks.

As with all persuasive investing stories, the arguments seemed obvious and were largely true. They also became incredibly simplified – the investment thesis supporting BRIC funds seemed to boil down to population and demographics. But while performance was strong, flimsy stories and increasingly expensive valuations didn't matter.

Investment stories don't just make things easier to understand, they make things easier to believe. We lose money on them because of the things we are not told or the things we do not see. The world is messy and unpredictable; the stories we are told are anything but. As fund investors we always need to remember that we are being told and sold a story. And they are hard to resist.

Do fund investors learn the wrong lessons about stories?

We might think that the BRIC fund debacle would at least allow investors to learn some lessons about the fickle nature of story-based investing. Surely, we would now understand that a good story is very often a poor investment. Unfortunately, not.

We learn lessons, just the wrong ones.

Rather than teach us about the danger of stories, we just move to a new, more compelling narrative.

BRICs and emerging markets became somewhere to avoid – chaotic, troubled and dangerous –, and the old straggler, the US, rose from the ashes of its lost decade to become the exceptional equity region. Emerging markets were forgotten, and the prevailing story moved to one about the dominant technology and new consumer companies in the US.

Why invest in anything else?

We cannot resist stories. They make disorderly and mercurial financial markets seem coherent, predictable and often exciting. Storytelling is part of the human condition. We will always be vulnerable to the next great investment tale, with asset managers its willing authors.

Instead of obsessing over the latest story, investors should be focusing on risk. I don't mean risk as in the volatility of our investment, but the danger of failing to meet our long-term goals. Investors can either fail quickly or slowly – we will find out how in the next chapter.

Ten-point fund investor checklist – stories

1. **What is the story supporting an investment?**

    All investment decisions are based on an underlying story. We must be clear about the narrative that is driving our decision.

2. **What is the past performance of that story?**

    Investment stories usually start with strong past performance. The stronger that past performance, the riskier our investment is likely to be.

3. **What is the valuation of the story?**

    The more expensive the securities related to a particular story, the more the story is already in the price.

4. **How reliant is the investment case on a particular story?**

    The more reliant an investment is on a particular narrative, the more downside risk there will be if it does not come to pass.

5. **How widely known is the story?**

    If a story is already widely known, we should ask ourselves what is it that we understand that other investors do not.

6. **How exciting and compelling is the story?**

    If a story is exciting and salient, we are increasingly vulnerable to poor decisions. The better the story sounds, the more cautious we should be.

7. **What is the main rationale for owning a thematic fund?**

    Popular thematic funds will almost inevitably have strong recent performance. When we invest we must be clear about what we think is not already understood by the market and priced accordingly.

8. **What is the track record of the thematic fund?**

    Thematic funds are particularly dangerous if they have delivered incredible past returns or have been recently launched after a successful backtest.

9. **When would we sell a thematic fund?**

   Most investments in thematic funds are an exercise in performance chasing/capturing price momentum. They are based on the assumption that the price will keep rising because the story is strong. This is a perfectly reasonable (if risky) approach to investing, but it is critical to plan when we would exit the fund in advance.

10. **How exposed are we to a single story?**

   Investing in funds because of a particular investing story or in high-risk thematic funds is only acceptable if it represents a fraction of our portfolio. Could we survive a 70–80% loss?

CHAPTER 6

INVESTMENT RISK IS NOT VOLATILITY; IT IS DISASTER AND DISAPPOINTMENT

THE ASSET MANAGEMENT industry loves to quantify risk. As we have seen, volatility has become the dominant measure, but terms such as 'maximum drawdown', 'beta' and 'tracking error' are also commonly used. The problem is that although these metrics are ubiquitous, they don't really tell us much about the real risks fund investors face.

Investment risk doesn't need complex formulas. At its heart it is a simple idea – it is the chance that we fail to meet our objectives.

Investment risk is the gap between what we hope to achieve and the actual result.

There are myriad ways in which investment risk can be realised, but they can all be split into two categories: disasters or disappointments.

We can either fail quickly or slowly.

The good news is that if we understand these risks, we can reduce them and materially improve the probability of enjoying good outcomes.

In this chapter I look to re-frame how we think about investment risk. I explore the twin dangers of concentrated funds, the true purpose of fund diversification and the slow, hidden killer that is negative compounding.

Let's start by looking at the dangers of what we do own and the dangers of what we don't.

What are the risks of concentrated funds?

In 2018 acclaimed Edinburgh-based active fund manager Baillie Gifford published an article entitled 'The Pursuit of Extreme Returns'.[1] The central tenet of the piece was that the long-run returns of equities have historically been produced by a very narrow group of companies. It cited research by Hendrik Bessembinder showing that although stocks overall outperformed government bonds across a 90-year period, the vast majority underperformed.[2]

It was the disproportionate impact of certain exceptional companies that dominated returns. The article goes on to claim that only 4.3% of firms collectively accounted for the creation of wealth in the US equity market between 1926 and 2016.

Somewhat inevitably – given their pedigree as an active, concentrated stock picker – the thrust of the argument put forward by Baillie Gifford was this: why would you want to own the entire market when so few companies are actually responsible for the returns produced? Owning all the laggard stocks is a huge impediment to performance. We should focus on owning those with the potential to be extraordinary.

Intuitively, this argument feels right; but it is entirely wrong.

In fact, it is probably the strongest single argument for index fund investing that I have ever come across.

The conclusion drawn by Baillie Gifford is that funds should be concentrated into a narrow selection of underlying securities. This is the exact opposite of the view that should be formed, because of one glaring problem.

It is true that long-run equity returns are likely to be focused on a narrow group of companies, and with the benefit of hindsight it is easy to identify who they were. Unfortunately, we cannot invest in the rear-view mirror. To take advantage of the fact that only a select group of companies matter, we need to know who they are in advance.

That is truly heroic assumption.

Rather than highlight the benefit of holding a small number of securities, the research identifies a stark limitation. If we own a concentrated fund, then there is a good chance that we will end up not owning the stocks that come to dominate future equity returns. We become reliant on the fund manager we select being able to identify the exclusive group of companies that are remarkable from the thousands that are not.

The most prudent course of action is not to take the long-odds bet that we can find and stick with those companies, but rather adopt a diversified approach to ensure that we will have exposure to the right companies.

It is a game of roulette – do you want to spread your chips across the table, or bet everything on red 17?

Concentrated funds foster severe risks because of the potential cost of what they don't own and not just the securities they do hold.

If our fund is heavily biased to a select group of stocks, countries or themes, we are susceptible to both the disappointment of not holding the right companies through time and also the disaster of large, dramatic losses.

Why take the risk of a fund blowing up?

Very concentrated funds are almost always a sign of overconfidence. They reflect an exaggerated view of our own knowledge and ability to predict the future. A single missing piece of vital information or an unexpected economic development is all it takes to produce dreadful results.

Concentration means that our investments are always close to the precipice, waiting for what tomorrow will bring.

Examples of the painful consequences of concentrated exposures are not difficult to find. The esteemed Sequoia Fund – which was founded by protégés of Warren Buffett in the 1970s and built on his investing principles – held a stake in pharmaceutical firm Valeant which became worth over 30% of the fund. They became the single largest investor in the company.[3]

Across 2015 and 2016, Valeant stock plunged from a peak of $257 to just $9 per share after the company was hit by claims of accounting irregularities and price gouging.[4] This savaged the previously strong long-term performance track record of the Sequoia Fund and left more recent investors facing steep losses.[5] Performance from other stocks held by the fund during this tumultuous period were strong, but when you are that concentrated one poor decision can overwhelm many good ones.

Valeant share price

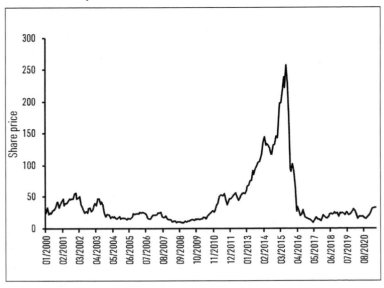

In a letter to Sequoia fund shareholders, the fund manager, David Poppe, stated:

> While we have beaten the market over the past decade, through

the end of 2015, our investment in Valeant has diminished a record that we have built over two generations and in which we take great pride.

This is what concentration does. It fosters an uncontrollable risk of disaster that can undo years, decades and generations of endeavour and gains. The risk is entirely unnecessary and the road back arduous. At the end of 2021, the Sequoia Fund's average annual return over ten years trailed the S&P 500 by over 3%.

Given the dangers of concentrated investing, why are fund managers willing to take such risks?

The most common argument for concentrated funds is often based on the notion that there is less risk in investing in 'what you know', but how true is this?

Is the argument for concentrated funds a myth?

Fund concentration can be about the number of positions in a portfolio (think of a stock portfolio with 20 or fewer holdings), the amount invested in one or more securities (more than 10% in a single position) or being narrowly exposed to a particular theme or idea (a clean energy ETF). It comes in many guises.

The key question is – how reliant is our investment success on a narrow range of positions? Could we still meet our objectives if they went wrong?

The risks from concentration are severe, but the asset management industry frequently extols its virtues. Why?

One argument is that in a landscape increasingly dominated by index funds surely active management only makes sense if a fund manager is focusing on the best opportunities? Otherwise just buy a cheap, diversified index fund. While there is some merit in this viewpoint, there is a material difference between a fund having a more focused approach than an index and being unnecessarily concentrated.

There is another more philosophical reason for fund concentration, which is founded on the notion that it actually reduces risk. How could this be the case?

If a fund manager invests in a small number of positions, we can be more confident in their ability to understand them. An equity manager can cover 20 companies with far greater rigour than 100. Warren Buffett is an understandable advocate of focused, high conviction investing; noting that it can enhance "both the intensity with which an investor thinks about a business and the comfort-level (s)he must feel with its economic characteristics."

Buffett's statement is incontrovertibly true. Unfortunately, it does not follow that it is a good strategy for most investors to pursue or that it reduces risk. Quite the contrary. More information can lead to a far greater risk of disaster.

In a 2008 study a group of researchers looked at the impact that an increasing amount of information had on the ability of an individual to predict the result of US college football games.[6]

Participants in the study had to forecast a winner for several games based on a selection of information about the teams involved. The information came in blocks of six (so for the first round of predictions the participant had six pieces of data) and after each round of predictions they were given another block of information, up to five blocks (or 30 data points) and had to update their views.

Participants were asked to predict both the winner and their confidence in their judgement between 50% and 100%. The aim of the experiment was to understand how increasing information impacted both accuracy and confidence.

And what were the results?

The additional information had a significant impact on the participants. But not on their accuracy, only their confidence. The quality of the forecasts flatlined, but the participants' belief that they were going to be correct rose. This result mirrored an unpublished study by Paul Slovic which, in a similar fashion, looked at the impact of increasing information on the ability of horse racing handicappers to pick winners.[7]

Sometimes knowing more gives us nothing but a false sense of certainty about unpredictable outcomes.

More information, worse decisions

It can seem puzzling that more information can be a disadvantage, but there are four specific ways in which information does nothing but erroneously increase our confidence:

- **When it is noise**

  What we believe to be information can be meaningless noise. This is where random data has no relevance and provides no insights, but we think it does. The more uncertainty there is in an activity, the more of a problem noise can be. Past performance of mutual funds is a good example of this; what we perceive to be information is often just the random fluctuations of financial markets.

- **When it is a duplicate**

  While there is some advantage to corroborating evidence, the most valuable piece of information is something that is new. In a trial, a sixth witness testifying that they saw the defendant at the scene of the crime is of minimal benefit. A fresh piece of information – fingerprints on a murder weapon, for example – should have a much more profound impact on our judgements.

- **When the most important information is missing**

  Swathes of information can lead us to forget what we do not know. For all the information that we do possess we might be missing the crucial piece. If we own the stock of a company and have intimate knowledge of its business practices and economics, it may give us great confidence in our investment; but what we do not know is that the CFO is engaged in fraud – this renders all other information close to worthless.

- **When it increases our commitment**

  The more effort we expend on something, the more committed we become to it. The greater our endeavour to procure additional information, the more valuable it seems.

For any activity – such as investing in companies and funds – where the information is incomplete and there is a high degree of unpredictability in future outcomes, we quickly reach the limit of knowledge. This is where (absent a crystal ball) we cannot reduce uncertainty further; additional information does not negate the fact that the future is unknowable.

There are always pieces of information that are hidden, obscured or misinterpreted. We never have the complete picture. This means that no matter how much we think we know, concentration always risks disaster from the misunderstood or the unknowable.

It always pays to diversify.

What's the point of diversification?

Diversification is often called 'the only free lunch' in investing. The concept is based on the generally sound principle that by investing in a range of securities, funds and asset classes with different characteristics we can reduce the risks that we face without impairing our return prospects (we might even improve them).

Diversification is both simpler and more important than this description suggests.

While diversification is now typically discussed in terms of correlations and volatilities, it is really about confidence. Diversifying our investments is an acceptance that we cannot predict the future and that we will be wrong about many things.

The more confident we are, the more concentrated our investments. With perfect foresight we would only invest in one security.

If we want to understand an investor's confidence, we need to check their diversification.

Diversification is not easy

Diversification is behaviourally challenging for fund investors for two reasons:

1. We will always be holding onto funds that are performing relatively poorly.

2. We are forced into making decisions that we think will be wrong.

Let's explain why:

Assume we own two funds investing in global equities. One is invested in large businesses, with rapidly growing earnings, the other in small value stocks. Given the distinct nature of these investments, they should provide some diversification benefits. A period in the sun for cheap and small companies will likely mean struggles for their larger, rapidly growing counterparts.

When our small cap value fund is outperforming, how do we feel?

Probably frustrated. Frustrated at the disappointing performance of the large company fund we hold. Questioning why we didn't and don't own more of the small company fund. Because it is underperforming it will be easy to find problems with the large strategy and simple to justify removing or reducing it.

To be appropriately diversified it is not enough for us to be happy to hold things that feel like they are not performing; we must want them not to work.

If all the funds in our portfolio are going up at the same rate at the same time, we have a problem. It just won't feel like a problem until it's too late.

Happy being wrong

Good investing is often framed as being about the avoidance of mistakes. While this is true in some regards, prudent diversification means being comfortable making decisions that we think will look like mistakes. When investing in the large and small company funds, we will inevitably have a preference between the two. We will likely hold an expectation about one fund being able to produce higher returns than the other. Despite this we should invest in both – because we are fallible, and the future is unknowable.

Appropriate diversification means always holding some assets and funds that appear to be stragglers. This is the intended result. We can think of such positions as failures or costs. Alternatively, we can consider them to be holdings that would have fared better in a different scenario to the one which transpired.

Diversifying our risks appropriately is challenging because it forces us to make decisions not only that we *think* are likely to be wrong and costly, but that we *want* to be wrong and costly.

This is difficult to justify to ourselves, let alone others.

A bet about diversification and confidence

Let's make a bet. There is £100,000 on offer. We must decide what will produce the highest return over the next decade – an emerging market equity fund or a US equity fund. We must allocate the £100,000 between the two options. We will receive the amount we stake on the strongest market.

If we are supremely confident, we can put it on a single outcome and risk losing the entire amount. If we are unsure, we can split it equally and guarantee £50,000.

Most investors will have a view on this choice. Some more forthright than others. If we had a strong disposition towards US equities, how aggressive would our stake be? Given the huge uncertainty surrounding the result, it makes little sense to go all in. We need to diversify and put money on both. This means allocating money to something that we think is wrong and want to be wrong. It is sensible and prudent, but uncomfortable.

If we wager £70,000 on US equities and they outstrip emerging market equities, how do we feel? We are likely to curse our conservatism, rather than think about the other possible paths taken. We were right, so why didn't we back ourselves more?

After the event, diversification only feels gratifying if we were wrong. If we were right it feels like a cost. If we bet each way on a horse that wins a race, we will rue the fact that we didn't bet solely on a victory.

Our struggle to appropriately diversify is related to loss aversion:

our tendency to experience the pain of losses more acutely than the pleasure of commensurate gains. This behavioural trait fosters a propensity to view diversification through a negative lens, focusing on the funds that failed to perform, rather than those that did.

Changing our minds

As always, the most challenging aspects of these types of decision are when they involve changing our mind. Let's expand on the emerging market versus US equities bet.

Imagine we are five years into the decade-long bet and we are asked if we want to adjust our stakes. We now have slightly less confidence in the prospects for US equities, and therefore alter our bet to £60,000 US/£40,000 emerging markets to reflect this change of view.

We have just made a decision that we want to be wrong. At the end of the ten-year period, it is in our interests if we were to look back and regret making this choice. We prefer US equities but are reducing our bet. We want it to cost us money. The level of cognitive dissonance here is pronounced.

When we make an investment decision there are a huge range of potential, unknowable paths. After the event, only one route has been taken and a binary judgement will be made – were we right or wrong? To make matters worse, everyone now feels that the result was obvious at the time we made our decision.

Diversification is much harder than it looks.

How to avoid disaster

The risk of disaster is always an issue of diversification. Even if we invest in a fund that turns out to be a fraud, if it is only 3% of our overall portfolio the consequences are likely to be bearable. How diversified we choose to be is about both our capacity for loss and our confidence in our investment judgement.

Thinking about the risk of disaster is problematic because it doesn't fit into the traditional risk and return framework within which the fund industry operates. Indeed, the concept that more risk should result in greater returns is flawed and dangerous when assessing the threat of large and disastrous losses.

There is no 'right' level of diversification; it is dependent on the requirements and characteristics of each individual. Diversification is no panacea. However, investors should assume that the more confident and concentrated we are, the greater the risk of disaster.

The risks from concentrated funds can be extreme and stark. There are other risks that are slow and creeping but can be just as damaging.

What is negative compounding?

Perhaps apocryphally, Albert Einstein called compound interest the eighth wonder of the world. Whatever the veracity around the origin of this comment, the sentiment is valid. Earning interest upon interest through time has a staggeringly powerful impact on our results. One that can often go unnoticed.

If we make an investment of £100,000 that will provide 5% interest per annum for 20 years and decide to reinvest the 5% annual interest, we will end the period with £265,329, a 165% gain. If instead we withdraw the interest each year, we will finish with just £200,000, a 100% gain.

Crucially, the gulf between the two approaches widens through time. If we are reinvesting, the profit we make in the final year is £12,635; if we are withdrawing it remains £5,000. That is a yawning 153% difference.

5% per annum return – reinvestment and withdrawal

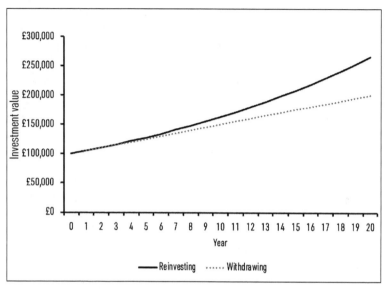

The power and danger of compounding is that it is a slow and largely hidden force, exerting its influence over years and decades. The attention span of investors is usually weeks or months, and our focus is drawn to the latest piece of economic news or market trend. We make trading decisions in an attempt (usually a hopeless one) to improve our returns, neglecting the fact that most of the work could be done for us. The profits we hope to make with our investment activity will likely be dwarfed by having a sensible appreciation of the influence of compounding.

The major risk of disappointment that fund investors face is not compounding as we might conventionally consider it, but the spectre of negative compounding: the small withdrawals or losses we make through time that reduce the amount of capital upon which we generate subsequent returns and earn interest. These can seem minor in any given year but build to have severe consequences. We lose money so slowly, we barely notice.

Maximising income and minimising returns

Fund investors have an affinity with investments that pay them a regular income; there seems to be an ingrained attraction to the tangible nature of dividends and coupons. Indeed, if they are reinvested then they will likely become the dominant driver of our long-term gains. Challenges arise, however, when we take income withdrawals from our portfolios. As interest rates fell investors increasingly looked towards equity and bond funds to meet their income requirements. And many asset managers were happy to make lofty promises about the amount of income that can be generated.

The central problem with such offerings is that income yields offered are often higher than the total returns that can be generated. This means that not only do we not have any income to reinvest and compound (because we have withdrawn it) but the value of our fund holding is decreasing through time, as are the income payments it produces.

If we have a fund that will return 4% per year for the next 25 years, what is the impact on income payments and capital values for an investor withdrawing 5% each year and another taking 3.5%?

Impact of 5% and 3.5% income withdrawals

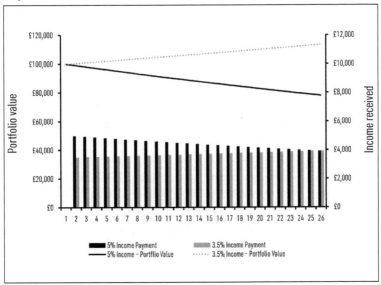

After 25 years there is a significant difference in the portfolio values. The investor withdrawing 3.5% is £35,000 better off, both because of the differing size of the withdrawal and the negative compounding of the high withdrawal – think of it as returns not earned because they were not reinvested. Even if we account for the income paid out, the investor receiving the lower yield is better off by £17,365.

Crucially, the influence of negative compounding means that by year 25 the investor with the lower income requirement is now receiving a higher income payout, because the value of their portfolio is greater. Their income has grown, while the high income investor's has declined.

It is imperative that we are acutely aware of the elevated income yield promises that asset managers tend to make about the funds they offer. The yield numbers used to sell funds can sometimes be detrimental to the results delivered. The long-term consequences from both a capital and income perspective can be significant and far more important than the headline yield. The erosion from negative compounding can be severe.

Of course, many of us require an income from our investments, but we must not neglect the potential impact of the level of income withdrawn and instead identify the least punitive way of securing it. Our efforts to maximise our near-term yield can easily minimise our gains and income over the long run.

Even for investors that are not interested in receiving an income, the spectre of negative compounding looms large.

Understanding the cost of active management

Although the money that we remove from fund investments can be costly, such costs are often unavoidable necessities. We may be able to manage them in a more effective manner to mitigate the effect of negative compounding, but most of us will have to draw on our investments at some juncture. We should aim to make withdrawals as small and as late as is feasible. Another crucial area to manage is the fees we pay for active management. Other things equal, the impact of seemingly modest fee differentials can grow into a substantial disparity as years pass.

When we think about active management fees we often compare the sticker price of two funds. Active Manager A costs 1% per year and Active Manager B 0.5%. This type of anodyne presentation can easily make us complacent about the true consequence of such a discrepancy. It avoids two crucial elements: a monetary comparison that makes the contrast more salient and, critically, time.

Negative compounding is about the passage of time. Snapshot fee comparisons can distract us from the real issues.

The true cost of fund fees is not about the cost differential between two funds over a given year. It is the interest and returns that we don't earn over time because of the additional fees that we have paid out.

If we assume the two funds both return 7% per annum over 20 years and the only difference is fees. How do the outcomes differ?

	Active Manager A	Active Manager B
Management Fee	1%	0.50%
Starting Value	£1,000,000	£1,000,000
Closing Value	£3,207,135.47	£3,523,645.06
Cumulative Return	220.70%	252.40%

When we let the negative compounding take hold over a long time period – 20 years in this case – the influence of fees and charges is significant. A 0.5% fee differential costs close to £316,510 from a £1,000,000 initial investment. The cumulative return difference is 32 percentage points.

It is also a cost that grows each year. It is a powerful force. For Active Manager A, the profit registered in the final year is £181,535 – 18% of the initial investment amount. For Active Manager B, the final year profit is £215,058 – 21% of the starting £1,000,000.

Annual gain relative to initial investment

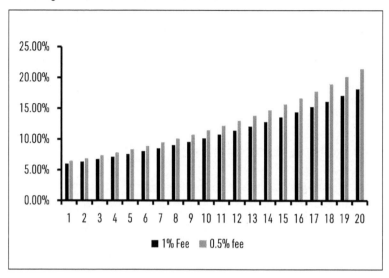

If we do nothing with our fund investment by the end of a 20-year period the annual gain is 3 percentage points greater than if we had selected the higher-fee active manager, such is the influence of negative compounding.

The example is somewhat unfair because it is founded on the assumption that there is no benefit from paying higher fees for Active Manager A. It is possible that we invest in a fund that can generate significantly greater returns than the cheaper option.

Outperformance is, however, uncertain and difficult to find. Contrastingly, fees are one of the few areas in investment that are within our control. All fund investors should seek to understand the cost of what they are investing in and whether it provides value for money.

The powerful impact of negative compounding over time is often obscured because over short periods its effect is barely noticeable and profoundly unexciting. Investment risks that cause long-run disappointment – such as negative compounding – are pernicious because it is easy to be blind to them. The near-term benefits are too small, and the long-term costs are too far into the future.

To mitigate the disappointment caused by negative compounding, investors need to minimise short-term costs. Active management fees is one area we can control but it is not the only one. There is another major return drag that fund investors bear, but it is not an explicit charge. Instead, it is an implicit behavioural tax that stems from our inability to resist the temptation put in our way by fluctuating fund performance.

How costly is performance chasing?

Negative compounding is not simply about the money we withdraw and the fees we pay, it is about the choices we make over time. Frequent, costly trading decisions act like an additional tax on our investments – with similar consequences to the other costs we incur. The most common and punitive behaviour of fund investors is performance chasing. Moving from underperforming funds to outperforming funds.

The price of this activity is penal.

The most damaging investment decisions tend to be those which make us feel good in the short term but come with a long-term cost. Where we look back and say: "I would have been better off doing nothing." Performance chasing in funds is a perfect example of this. Nobody enjoys paying an underperforming active manager, and our appetite to shift into a better performing competitor can be strong. The trouble is, switching between yesterday's winners and losers is a terrible strategy.

But just how costly is it?

A research paper produced by Vanguard compared the returns generated by a buy and hold fund investment strategy with one that switched from funds that lagged over three years to those that had outperformed. Their simulation incorporated 40 million different return paths and the results were stark. In all nine US equity styles studied, the returns from a buy and hold approach outstripped a performance chasing strategy. The average annual performance differential was 2.8%.[8]

These findings are consistent with another study published in *The Journal of Portfolio Management*, which assessed the performance of over 3,000 funds between 1994 and 2016. It found that, on a three-year time horizon, recent winners had worse future performance than funds with losing track records.[9]

What are the causes of the cost of performance chasing? There are three drivers:

1. **Mean reversion**

   The main trigger is likely to be mean reversion, where outperforming funds simply generate unsustainable returns. If we think a highly skilled fund manager can deliver outperformance of 2% per annum, and then invest in an active fund following a prolonged period when they have produced excess returns of 6% per annum, we are very likely to bear the pain of performance coming back down to earth.

2. **Investor sentiment**

   Funds with significant outperformance are likely to be operating in areas of the market with strongly positive investor sentiment and persistently high inflows. If the mood changes, this situation can reverse dramatically.

3. **Valuations**

   The securities held in an outperforming fund are also more likely to be expensive and therefore produce lower future returns, with the reverse being true for underperformers.

Unusually strong performance, ebullient investor sentiment and high valuations is a toxic combination and renders performance chasing a behavioural tax compounding into a huge long-term disadvantage. And one that we are unlikely to notice until it is too late.

How should fund investors think about risk?

Fund investors have been conditioned to think about risk in the wrong way. We typically consider it as the general volatility of returns, but this is misleading. Almost all the risks we encounter can be defined as rapid, high impact disasters, or creeping and corrosive disappointments.

	Disasters	Disappointment
Speed	Fast	Slow
Salience	High	Low
Visibility	High	Low
Magnitude	High	High

The narrow fashion in which we conceptualise risk leaves us sharply vulnerable to both disaster and disappointment, and the overarching risk of failing to meet our objectives. The good news for fund investors is that with careful consideration and planning most of these risks are well within our control.

If we better understand the risks, we really can reduce them and improve our returns.

One of the major problems that fund investors face is that they set themselves up for disaster and disappointment from the very beginning. How do they do this? By selecting funds based on past performance. There is no worse way to choose a fund, and the next chapter will show why.

Ten-point fund investor checklist – disaster and disappointment

1. **How concentrated is the fund?**

   Investing in concentrated funds is a high-risk strategy. It is only acceptable if they are held as part of a diversified portfolio. A combination of concentrated funds can make for a sensibly diversified blend of risks.

2. **Could we survive a blow-up?**

   If one stock or area of the market went badly wrong, could our portfolio withstand this?

3. **What don't we own?**

   Concentration risk is as much about what we don't own as what we do. The more concentrated we are, the more we are vulnerable to strong performance from areas of the market that we do not hold.

4. **Are we really diversified?**

   It is easy to appear diversified by owning multiple funds, but if all of these funds invest in similar areas or are exposed to consistent themes we still carry considerable concentration risk.

5. **Is our level of diversification consistent with our confidence?**

   Diversification is about confidence. The more concentrated and undiversified we are, the more confident about our investment views we must be.

6. **How much income do we really need?**

   Withdrawing income is a drag on our long-term returns; we should only take what we require and no more.

7. **Do we need to take income?**

   Depending on taxation, it can be beneficial to create an income by drawing down on capital (selling units in a fund) rather than receiving a natural income. This also makes it easier to manage the size of withdrawals.

129

8. **How much are we paying in fees and why?**

It is important to know not only how much we are paying in fees but also what we are paying them for.

9. **Are we making decisions based on past performance?**

Performance chasing – selling losers and buying winners – is a painful tax paid by fund investors.

10. **How extreme are performance, valuations and sentiment for the funds we are buying and selling?**

This trifecta of factors makes performance chasing incredibly costly.

CHAPTER 7

PAST PERFORMANCE IS A TERRIBLE WAY TO SELECT A FUND

I N THE PREVIOUS chapter I showed an example of the cost of performance chasing in funds. Selling underperformers and buying outperforming funds is a behavioural tax for investors. A decision that makes us feel good at the time, but which comes at a significant long-term cost.

Despite the dangers, most fund investors still only buy funds with strong recent performance. Our preferred metric for selecting funds puts the odds against us right from the start.

Why do we make such a severe mistake, and what can we do about it?

This chapter is an exploration of the perils of making fund selection decisions based on past performance. I begin by studying the problem of outcome bias and why past performance is irresistible. I then highlight two cardinal sins of performance-driven fund investing: using performance screens and trusting backtests. I close by presenting a framework for how fund investors should approach the challenge of separating luck and skill, so we can finally move away from the obsession with past performance.

But let's begin with a game of cricket.

What has cricket got to do with fund investing?

Cricket is a wonderfully arcane activity. It is the second most popular sport in the world (largely thanks to India) but is typically only widely played in countries that bear the footprint of British colonialism. To the uninitiated it is a ridiculous, inexplicable game full of eccentricities. Some matches can last for five days and still end in a draw.

How does it bear any relevance to fund investing?

Sport is the home of outcome bias. The domain in which most of us regularly make judgements based solely on the result, despite the pronounced role of luck. The assessments we make about players, coaches and teams is always inexorably linked to success or failure, irrespective of how it was achieved. Much like our judgements of funds.

In 2019, England won the Cricket World Cup and outcome bias ran amok. Rest assured, you don't need to understand the game to understand the principle.

Before England's 2019 success, the Cricket World Cup had been held 11 times, beginning in 1975 and running approximately every four years. Despite being one of the pre-eminent teams, England had never won the tournament but had finished runners-up on three occasions.

The 2015 World Cup saw a particularly dispiriting and ignominious exit for the England team, which brought about an overhaul of their approach to the game. An ambitious four-year plan to win the trophy when the competition returned to home shores in 2019 was forged.

Although England did indeed win the 2019 Cricket World Cup after overcoming New Zealand in the final, it is unlikely that this would have happened were it not for an outrageous slice of good fortune.

Without going into any unnecessary detail; extremely late in the game a ball took a wicked deflection off an England batsman after being thrown by a New Zealand player, which resulted in England being gifted extra runs through nothing but sheer chance.

Absent this incident England would probably not have lifted the trophy. While all sport is to an extent defined by luck and randomness, it is worth highlighting that every ex-professional cricketer I have heard discuss this incident said that they had never seen such a thing happen before. For it to transpire in such a pivotal match at such an important stage of the game is delightfully ridiculous.

It is not fair to say that England were lucky to win the World Cup – there was a great deal of skill that got them to the position to win the competition – rather they would have been unlikely to do so without the assistance of an unprecedented freak occurrence.

Following England's victory, the immediate and persuasive narrative was:

- The meticulous four-year plan to transform the game was an incredible success.

- The team fully justified their pre-tournament favourites tag.

- The players were able to handle the pressure of a World Cup final.

These points all have a level of validity, but England probably only won the game because of a once-in-a-lifetime piece of luck – what if everything had been the same, but that incredible deflection had not occurred? What would the prevailing narrative have been then?

- England's four-year plan failed as they lose yet another final.

- The team didn't live up to their billing as pre-tournament favourites.

- They didn't cope with the pressure of a World Cup Final.

The bounce of a ball not only changed the result of a cricket tournament and the lives of the England players, but it also framed our perception of everything that led to that victory.

This is an absurd situation. The assessment of a detailed four-year plan cannot hinge on the random deflection of a ball; but this is the very nature of outcome bias – we take the result and then work back, viewing everything through the lens of that outcome. Taking such an approach in activities where there is luck and randomness involved is hopelessly flawed. We seem to operate a binary narrative switch, which will flick between two entirely contradictory rationales depending on the result.

In my experience outcome bias is one of our most intractable failings. Trying to persuade anybody to look past the result and consider the quality of the process underpinning it is nigh on impossible. You often look foolish even suggesting it.

Outcome bias is the most influential behavioural weakness in fund investing.

Why are we obsessed with past performance?

Why does the Cricket World Cup matter to investors?

Most sports are dominated by skill but punctuated with doses of luck. In many cases outcomes are a reasonable proxy for the quality of a process. Those with skill are likely to enjoy success.

For fund investment the reverse is true: it is luck and randomness with an element of skill. This means we should be even more leery of outcomes alone telling us something meaningful, but, if anything, we are more reliant. Performance frames and overwhelms virtually all investment activity and decision making. We are obsessed by the name on the trophy and care far too little about how it got there.

As fund investors, past performance dominates our judgements because we assume that it must be an indicator of skill. We struggle with the cognitive dissonance of a talented fund manager underperforming – if they had talent, surely they would be beating the market?

Luck and randomness mean that this will often not be the case.

To better show the impact of randomness, I created a simulation. I took 300 'funds' and ran them over ten discrete calendar year periods. Every year each fund was ascribed a return at random. This could be +3%, +2%, +1%, 0, –1%, –2%, –3%. At the end of the ten years, the 300 funds would have a cumulative total return based on the compounding of the ten random annual returns they were given. The distribution of results is shown in the next chart.

Performance of 300 random 'funds'

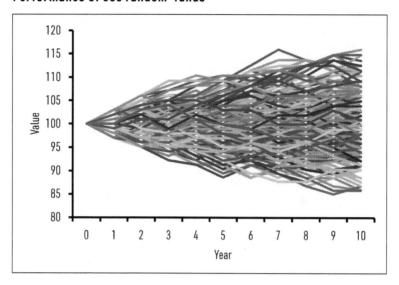

Each line represents a return path taken by one of the 300 funds. While a normal distribution is to be expected, what is critical is the pattern of returns for each. Despite being allocated random performance numbers with an equal chance of positive or negative returns, there were still significant streaks of performance. Some 21% of the 300 funds enjoyed three consecutive years of positive returns, while 11% had runs of four years or more. Even when the results are pure randomness, we still get periods of consistent returns the likes of which fund investors so often ascribe to skilful or star fund managers.

Headline returns alone tell us very little. To find a skilful active fund manager, we need to do much more than look at past performance. When we rely on performance to inform our fund investment decisions we have no means of judging whether it is just a consequence of sheer chance.

Many investors seem aware that strong fund performance is often fleeting and rarely persists from one period to the next. Yet they continue to consciously or sub-consciously let historic returns drive their decisions to buy and sell a fund.[1]

135

Why do they do this?

There are two crucial reasons. One is that a focus on performance is a self-perpetuating norm and the other is that using outcomes as a gauge of skill serves us very well in many aspects of our lives.

Let's take each in turn.

Everybody else is doing it, so must I

For most fund investors – particularly those employed to pick funds – knowing that past performance can be a poor and erratic guide to future returns is irrelevant. What matters is what other people think. If everyone else believes in the information provided by historic results, then so must we. The famous John Maynard Keynes dictum applies here: it is far better to fail conventionally. Investing in an underperforming fund simply carries too much risk.

If we invest in an active fund that has a glittering track record, then the cost to our reputation if it goes on to disappoint is low. The strong historic results will be taken as an indication of the manager's talent and many others will be invested alongside us. Our decision to buy the fund was entirely understandable; the underperformance was mere bad fortune and we were not alone in suffering it.

Conversely, investing in a fund that was already performing poorly is unconscionable. It will be viewed as obvious that the fund was failing at the time we invested; why were we going in while everybody else was heading for the exit? It won't look like bad luck; it will look like a terrible decision made in spite of the evidence.

Although investing in a strongly performing fund often carries more risk from a pure investment standpoint, from a personal and reputation perspective all the risk resides with selecting the laggard.

Past performance matters because everybody else thinks it does.

It is not that outcomes are unimportant for investors. Of course the end result that we achieve is the most important thing. But positive performance outcomes should be a consequence of our investment decision making, not an input. The mistake we make is to assume that using outcomes as a proxy for skill works in investment as it does in other areas of our life.

Unfortunately, that is far from the truth.

The outcome heuristic

Outcomes or past results are only useful indicators of talent if an activity is dominated by skill. Take chess as an example. It is a heavily structured game reliant on skill, not chance, with limited luck and randomness in its results. If I played 100 chess matches with Grandmaster Magnus Carlsen, I would lose each one and these outcomes would prove an excellent indication of our relative abilities. We wouldn't need to watch each match to know this. Using outcomes as a quick heuristic here is perfectly efficient and effective.

Now imagine that I had to enter a portfolio management competition against my nine-year-old daughter, where we each had to pick our favourite fund in an asset class. As much as I might like to believe that I would hold a significant advantage, I know the probability of my selections outperforming hers over a single year are not much greater than 50%. While the odds may tilt in my favour as the time horizon extends, there are no guarantees – maybe she liked the name of a fund that goes on to enjoy incredibly strong performance, or inadvertently picks a fund with a style that is in vogue for several years. I am faced with the prospect of my diligent investment decision making being improved upon by the haphazard selections of a child.

The problem we face is that in many domains, using outcomes as a heuristic for a good process is a sensible and economical approach. But when randomness exerts a considerable influence it is grossly misleading.

We use outcomes as a rule of thumb in fund selection not only because we do it in everyday life but because it makes a highly complex and inherently challenging task easier. Disentangling and understanding the factors that lead to strong future fund performance is incredibly difficult and doesn't guarantee success even if we do it well. It is far simpler to assume that past outcomes are telling us all we need to know.

This view is so entrenched in fund investing that we let past performance overwhelm every aspect of our decision making; it influences our thinking right from the start.

What is the problem with performance screens?

One of the main challenges faced by fund investors is that we are presented with a baffling array of options. It seems impossible to diligently assess the thousands of available choices. A quick and easy way to narrow the fund universe is essential.

What is the most common way of doing this? Using a performance screen.

A performance screen is a simple means of filtering a potential opportunity set. We take the asset class we want to invest in (let's say US equities) and then use a performance database (such as Lipper or Morningstar) to sort the funds available.

Although this seems a reasonable solution, there is a problem. The popular method of ranking funds in such a screen is based on past performance. Different types of investors will use different measures. Some will simply order based on the highest returns over a given period, some will use performance consistency (how many periods they have outperformed), and others will employ seemingly more sophisticated approaches using risk-adjusted measures such as information ratios.

The level of complexity doesn't really matter; everyone is essentially doing the same thing – searching for funds with strong past performance and discarding those without it.

This is a ubiquitous and terrible idea.

Performance screens are a deeply flawed approach to filtering a universe of funds. To believe they are of merit, we must accept that historic performance alone gives us information about the skill of a manager and that strong historic returns are persistent.

Neither of these claims is true.

Past performance alone tells us nothing about whether a fund manager is skilful or lucky, and we know that chasing strong historic performance is a poor strategy.

The challenge of disregarding performance screens is that it leaves us with a major headache. How do we limit the range of fund options we have available to us?

There are a few paths we can take:

1. **Use other metrics**

   We don't have to use performance. A universe of funds can be filtered by using other metrics that are not focused on past performance. We can identify measures that we believe are important to successful fund management and use those to reduce our opportunity set. These could be the level of assets under management (not too large or too small), the tenure of the manager (we want a manager with a certain level of experience) and the active share of a fund (how different it is from an index fund option).

2. **Screen for poor performers**

   This may seem heretical, but as there is evidence that funds with strong recent returns go on to struggle, we should instead look at those funds going through a difficult spell. The most attractive opportunities are likely to be in funds run by skilful managers but enduring a period of underperformance.

3. **Invest in index funds**

   If we have no reasonable means of narrowing the universe of funds, and don't have the time to assess the full spectrum of alternatives, then we should be investing in index funds. This is far better than ingraining performance chasing behaviour by using screens.

It is not that performance screens are simply ineffective; it is that they are an objectively poor means of selecting funds. We would be better off picking names out of a hat.

Given what we know about how misleading and dangerous performance chasing can be, the widespread use of performance screens seems perverse. It is not, however, the most puzzling aspect of how fund investors revere performance. That would be backtests.

We make decisions to buy funds based on past performance even when it is made up.

Should we trust a fund's backtest?

One of the most grievous sins in fund selection is a reliance on backtests to justify investment in a fund.

A backtest is the hypothetical performance of a fund had it existed in the past and adopted the same process. Asset managers know that investors are reticent to invest in a fund that has no performance track record, so they create one. The inevitably glittering returns that are shown can lure investors in but can be worse than worthless.

Why are they so dangerous?

Because anyone can build a fund with a strong backtest.

If we wanted to create a new fund with strong backtested performance, we could take the previous ten years of financial market data and then run thousands of portfolio simulations based on different trading rules. We could then review the backtest results and select the rules that have generated the best risk-adjusted returns. We will then have successfully mined the data to produce both an investment process and a track record.

We don't need to hold a PhD in quantitative finance to see the problems here. If we run enough simulations then we are bound to find some combinations that result in attractive performance, even if they are all nothing but noise. Researchers call this "selection bias under multiple testing."[2] We show our potential investors only the most successful outcomes and discard all the failures.

The approach is analogous to a stock picking fraud. We take 100,000 people and separate them into 100 groups of 1,000 and send each group a different high-risk stock recommendation. Of the 100 stock tips, 90 fail and 10 deliver high returns. We now take the 10,000 people who received a lucrative stock market tip and split them into 100 groups of

100 people. Again, we send each group a new high-risk stock proposal. We can continue this process until we have ten people who have each received four astonishingly successful stock market tips.

Given that we have proven our otherworldly investing acumen, we can now ask the duped recipients for their money. They cannot see that 360 of our 400 recommendations have been abject failures, they are only aware of the successes. Although backtesting in funds is not as brazen a scheme as this, it does often rely on not showing investors the most critical pieces of information: the attempts that did not work.

Our chances of finding a winning formula are also greatly enhanced by our knowledge of what has happened in the past – what is often called data snooping. When designing a new fund, we are almost certain to know what investment factors or rules worked well during that period and can tilt our approach in that direction. This almost guarantees good results. Investment decisions are always easier to make in the past than the future.

The other major flaw of backtested fund performance is overfitting. This is where the parameters of our simulation are designed to fit or work well in the particular time that we are studying (so-called in-sample), even if the relationships identified are specific to that period of history. Entirely random data will show patterns and trends which can persuade investors that they are observing something more meaningful and permanent. Most times they are not. Overfitting is one of the main reasons why it is so common for a fund's backtested outperformance to evaporate as soon as it meets the real world.[3]

It seems absurd that investors would allocate money to funds with approaches constructed in such a fashion. Fund backtests will always show attractive performance. If they didn't, we would not be seeing it. We also never see the thousands of trials that produce poor results. It is akin to asking a fund manager to choose their own performance. It can be a marketing and sales exercise, rather than an investment one, and one which leads to frequent disappointment.

What can we do about backtests?

As fund investors we are complicit in the prevalence of funds launched and sold based on unfeasibly strong backtested performance. Our obsession with past performance means we want to see strong historic numbers, even if they are hypothetical and deeply flawed. Strong backtests can drive flows even if they don't drive future performance.[4]

We have a peculiar relationship with backtests. Most investors are sceptical of them but still let them influence investment decisions.

Who has ever invested in a fund with a poor backtest?

Most investors can entirely disregard backtests. The universe of funds with established live track records is so vast that there really is no need to become involved in fledgling, unproven strategies. Buying a fund based on realised past performance is problematic enough; investing because of hypothetical results can be even worse.

However, if a situation arises where we are considering investing in a fund that only has results from a backtest, there are several steps we can take to mitigate some of the most significant problems:

1. Ensure that there is a sound and independent rationale as to why the approach adopted should deliver excess returns. These could be behavioural or technical explanations, but it is essential to understand the likely causes of the anomalies that a fund is seeking to exploit.

2. Ask to see all the data that went into the development of the fund. Was there a clear starting hypothesis, or was it a case of data mining? How many different simulations were run? What were the results of these?

3. Understand over what period the data used in the backtest was generated. Has the process been tested in other environments?

4. Ascertain whether the backtest is a fair representation of the fund being managed live. Are trading costs accurately accounted for? If not, does the alpha still exist when all costs and real-world friction are included?

5. Identify whether results of similar strategies are available elsewhere. This could be from academic papers or other fund managers. It is highly unlikely that the fund we are considering has happened upon a unique investment approach and, if it has, we should ask ourselves why.

6. Set realistic expectations. If we are to invest in a fund with no live track record but strong backtested results, we should assume that the realised performance of the fund once launched will be significantly inferior to the backtest. Years of consistent and high returns in a backtest will not persist when a fund goes live. The more inconsistent the backtested results of a fund are with the lived experience of fund investing, the more concerned we should be with the process used to generate them.

Even adopting these measures won't fully protect us from the dangers of relying on backtested performance. It is critical to understand that the sale of investment funds based on positive backtests is a deliberate attempt to exploit our susceptibility to outcome bias. Our instinct to infer that a process is robust simply because its results are strong stretches to theoretical results generated with the benefit of hindsight.

The ability of backtests to beguile and mislead fund investors is the perfect example of our unhealthy fascination with past performance, but what can be done about it?

At its heart the problem is created by our inability to separate luck and skill. We just don't know how to assess the qualities of an active fund manager, so we use performance as a shorthand.

There is a better way, and to see this we need to return to the world of sport. This time it's football.

How can we tell a skilful fund manager from a lucky one?

Jurgen Klopp is one of the most revered football coaches of his generation. After success at both Mainz and Borussia Dortmund in Germany, he took the helm at Liverpool in October 2015. Since his appointment he has revived the fortunes of the moribund football superpower, leading them to their first English league title in 30 years and victory in the prestigious UEFA European Champions League.

Given the results he has delivered, nobody now doubts the wisdom of the club handing Klopp the reins; but there is something puzzling about Liverpool's hire. They made the decision following one of Klopp's most difficult seasons as a manager. In the four seasons between 2010 and 2014, Klopp's Borussia Dortmund side had won the league twice and finished as runners-up twice. In the 2014/2015 season, however, the team languished near the bottom of the table for its first half before recovering somewhat to finish in an underwhelming seventh place.

Football is a notoriously fickle sport. Fans and owners are impatient and have short memories. The average tenure of a manager in the English Premier League is less than two years (similar to our tolerance for fund manager underperformance). A poor season usually leaves a manager out of a job; in Klopp's case it led him to one of the most sought-after roles in the game.

What were Liverpool doing differently?

They were aware of luck. Specifically, they were aware of the influence of luck over short time horizons. A key pillar of Liverpool's recruitment process was the work of Ian Graham who, as head of research at the club, was tasked with developing football analytics. He produced mathematical models to assess the performance of teams and players, and predict the outcomes of games.

Based on an understanding of the factors that most prominently affect the results of football matches, Graham's work allowed for a systematic analysis of the difference between the actual result and the expected result based on the key statistics from a match, a gap that can be largely attributable to good or bad luck.

The work on Klopp showed that his struggling Dortmund side was incredibly unlucky.[5] From a statistical perspective, the performance of the team in the first half of the 2014/2015 season was not materially different from their prior successful seasons; it is just that the outcomes were much worse. As Graham noted: "We really thought that Dortmund had had bad luck. It wasn't anything to do with systematic problems with the players and the coach."[6]

It is difficult to overstate how good the decision Liverpool made with Klopp was. Not because of the success he has since delivered to the club, but because their approach ran counter to our behavioural tendencies. The common approach in the game is to obsess about recent results and make judgements based on small, biased samples.

Imagine the reaction if Klopp had failed at Liverpool – many would have claimed that it was obviously a poor appointment because he was already in decline at Borussia Dortmund.

In any activity where luck and randomness are involved it is crucial to be sceptical about using short-term results alone to influence decisions. Football is a game that is mainly skill complemented by a healthy dose of luck; investment and fund selection is the reverse. It is therefore even more important to disregard small noisy samples.

Liverpool were focused on whether Jurgen Klopp had skill, not whether recent results had been good.

Can fund investors follow this approach?

Think about the PROCESS

Consistent with Liverpool's search for a new coach, when we invest with an active fund manager we are trying to find skill – a manager that can deliver superior returns to other people and the aggregate results of other people (i.e., the market).

Given that focusing on outcomes alone is inadequate in an investment context, how should we approach locating skill in an activity where randomness heavily skews the results? Rather than focus on one element, there are seven important interrelated components that need to be considered: Path, Repetition, Objective, Calibration, Edge, Specification and Success (PROCESS).

I will explain each in turn utilising a golfing analogy – although I don't play the game, it is an activity that does incorporate both luck (less) and skill (more) and will hopefully serve to simplify the idea.

There are two golfers (Nelly and Lydia) and both have taken one shot at a par-3 hole and landed the ball close to the flag – let's say three feet away. How do we determine whether each player has golfing skill?

Path

Understanding the path (how a result was achieved) can give us far richer information. Nelly's shot went arrow straight at the flag. Lydia sliced her shot and it rebounded off a tree and onto the green. Given this new information, we are emboldened in our view that Nelly has skill, but now we are doubtful that Lydia does – it looks as if she has just enjoyed a significant slice of luck.

Repetition

Samples of one are never a good guide to skill, and the more randomness in an activity the more evidence we require. Although we might have a strong inclination that Nelly possesses greater skill, with only one example each we are incredibly vulnerable to being fooled by random occurrences.

Objective

It is very dangerous to assume that an individual has skill simply from observing an activity – if we don't understand what they were trying to achieve beforehand. If we knew that Nelly was attempting to hit her shot at the flag near which she landed her ball then we can have increased confidence that she possesses skill. But what if we knew that Lydia was actually attempting to hit her ball onto the green after ricocheting off a tree? Rather than believe that she had just been lucky, we might consider that she has superior skill to Nelly because she performed a more difficult task.

Calibration

All activities sit somewhere on the luck and skill continuum, and it is important to have a perspective on how much randomness and complexity there is in an activity before making any judgements about skill. For example, landing a plane is dominated by skill with a modicum of luck involved – if I witness an individual landing a plane successfully it gives me far greater confidence that they have skill in that task, than the confidence I might gain from watching Nelly hit a single good golf shot. Trying to correctly calibrate the randomness inherent in an activity helps us to understand how much value there might be in the outcomes alone.

Edge

We should always ask whether the skill matters. If it is something that everybody can do then identifying skill is not particularly noteworthy. Driving a car is a skill, but as many people possess that expertise it is not one that is difficult to obtain. If I witness a succession of golfers hit shots equally as good as Nelly and Lydia then it tells me that the skill is unremarkable.

Specification

When seeking to define skill, we need to be specific about the activity in which someone possesses it. Even if we witness both Nelly and Lydia repeat the exact same feat on numerous occasions, we can only be confident that they have skill in that precise task. We may infer that they are skilled golfers, but they might be terrible at making short putts, a particular aspect of the game about which we have no evidence.

Success

If we were simply judging outcomes alone we might say that both golfers possess skill, as they have both produced excellent results.

As we can see from this golfing example, understanding the different elements of the process can transform our view on whether we are observing skill or randomness. When we are considering buying an actively managed fund, rather than focus on past performance we need to attempt to identify skill by thinking about the process and asking these questions:

Path: How has the objective been reached?

Repetition: How often has this process led to the same outcome?

Objective: What is the objective of the activity?

Calibration: How much luck or randomness do we think is involved in the activity?

Edge: How difficult is the task?

Specification: What is the precise activity in which we are attempting to identify skill?

Success: What was the overall result?

Fund investors give pre-eminence to outcomes when determining skill. Even when we incorporate other factors, our perspective is often biased by the strong priors we develop after initially observing performance. If we see strong performance, we assume skill must be involved. We are also prone to assume that apparent skill in one specific aspect translates across the entire spectrum of investment activities. Someone is often considered a 'good/great investor' – good at what, exactly?

Although skewed incentives and our obsession with outcomes make it incredibly demanding, the only way to even attempt to successfully identify skill is to understand not what the outcomes were, but precisely how they have been achieved.

If we don't know how a manager is generating returns, we should not be investing.

How should we treat strong past performance?

Our preoccupation with past performance is a perplexing trait. Investing in a fund with strong historic returns means that we are often buying somebody else's alpha. Returns that other people have enjoyed, that make it less likely that we will experience future success.

It seems that the pull of outcome bias is so strong that we blithely ignore this unappealing fact and the dangers of buying funds based on impressive recent performance.

We should certainly continue to use strong past performance as an input when selecting a fund, but as a caution rather than a buy signal. The more extreme historic outperformance is, the more fearful we should be about future results.

Our fascination with past performance not only leads to poor returns but has helped to create a vast asset management industry that is not well aligned with its investors. The next chapter will explore how we came to be in such a disappointing situation.

Ten-point fund investor checklist – past performance

1. **What is the performance history of the fund we are buying?**

   Although we will often give other reasons, strong past performance is almost always the primary driver of our fund investment decisions.

2. **How strong has recent performance been?**

   The more stellar recent returns, the more likely they are to crash back down to earth.

3. **How dependent have historic returns been on the market environment?**

   Fund performance is often more about the market environment than the manager. If the environment changes, so does a manager's performance profile.

4. **Would we accept the fund underperforming by the amount it has outperformed?**

   If a fund outperforms by 20% we should expect it to underperform by 20%. If we cannot accept this, we should not invest.

5. **How did we find the fund?**

   If we used a performance screen, then we have started in entirely the wrong place.

6. **Are the fund's historic returns real or from a backtest?**

   All past performance is misleading, but backtests are especially so.

7. **What skill is possessed by the fund manager?**

   To stop obsessing over past performance, we must instead focus on what skill the manager has.

8. **Is it possible to find evidence of that skill?**

   Skill is about a repeated link between process and outcomes. To invest in an active fund we need to define that skill and see consistent evidence of it in action.

9. **Have we ever bought a fund with poor recent performance?**

   Fund investors rarely buy funds with disappointing recent track records.

10. **Are we appropriately diversified?**

    If we only invest in funds with strong track records we are likely to become increasingly concentrated in funds with the same styles and biases. We will be far less diversified than we think we are.

CHAPTER 8

THE INCENTIVES OF ASSET MANAGERS ARE NOT ALIGNED WITH THEIR INVESTORS

THE ASSET MANAGEMENT industry has an incentive problem. The imperative to raise assets and maximise short-term profits means that managers' motives can be in stark contrast to our best interests.

The incentive structure of asset management businesses can facilitate and even promote our most damaging behaviours: short-termism, unnecessarily high turnover and chasing the next investment fad. Poorly designed incentives can lead fund managers to diverge from their stated investment philosophy, delivering them huge rewards despite tepid performance.

In this chapter I explore the problem with the asset management business model and show why it can be structured to work against fund investors. I then consider the incentive alignment of fund managers and why the often proposed solutions of performance fees and co-investment are no panacea. I close by outlining the changes that are needed for the industry to better serve its customers.

But before discussing asset managers, we will look at a rat infestation in early twentieth century Hanoi.

What can rats in Hanoi teach us about asset manager incentives?

In 1902 Hanoi was under French colonial occupation. As is so often the hallmark of empire, there were two sides to the city: a French Quarter of luxury villas and wide avenues for the colonists, and cramped, less salubrious conditions in the Old Quarter, home to the Vietnamese. Some 90% of the population was crammed into one-third of the surface area.[1]

Under the leadership of Paul Doumer, future president of France, the French had strived to bring European 'progress' and infrastructure to Hanoi. This included fresh water and a sewerage system. Nine miles of pipework were laid underneath the city with, of course, superior provision for the French Quarter. This symbol of modernity, however, had a disconcerting side-effect.

This dark and damp network of tunnels provided the perfect home and highway for the rodent community. Rats had direct access to the homes of the wealthy inhabitants of Hanoi. Stories abound of the creatures emerging from toilets and overflow pipes.[2]

It wasn't just unpleasantness and uncleanliness that prompted uproar; outbreaks of the bubonic plague were being reported across Asia, and the rats were suspected of carrying the disease. Action had to be taken to halt the infestation.

Initially the government tasked sewer workers with hunting the rats, but they understandably baulked at the disagreeable and dangerous task. Instead, in a stroke of seeming ingenuity, a bounty was placed on each rat; anyone who killed one would be paid a small amount. This incentivised the population – particularly the poor – to assist in the effort of bringing a halt to the rat epidemic.

The results were impressive. In early May 1902 more than 4,000 rats were killed each day, and this was just the start. On 21 June over 20,000 rats were killed.[3] The scheme seemed to be an astounding success.

But there was a problem.

Although the number of rats being killed was high and growing, the number of rats being seen on the streets – and in homes – did not seem to be declining. And there was something else. There were increasing sightings of rats without their tails.

It is here we come to the incentive problem.

To earn a reward for vanquishing a rat, its tail had to be taken to the municipal office (the government understandably was not keen on collecting the dead bodies). The incentive set seemed sensible and consistent with the overall objective of reducing the rat population, but it was not. The actual incentive was twofold: to harvest rats' tails and increase the number of rats in Hanoi, which had become a valuable commodity.

The impressive initial death toll that seemed to validate the plan was an illusion. The system was being gamed because the incentives were misaligned. There was evidence of rats being farmed within the city and even smuggled in from outside. An apparently sensible incentive served to exacerbate the problem it was designed to solve.

Why does a tale of rats' tails in early twentieth century Vietnam matter? Because it exemplifies how incentives drive our behaviour. If there is conflict between what we are trying to achieve and how people are being rewarded, it is the latter that will win out.

For fund investors it is easy to ignore how our aims can be at odds with the incentives of the asset managers with which we invest, but we do this at our peril.

The asset management model can be misaligned with its investors

> Never, ever, think about something else when you should be thinking about the power of incentives.
>
> **–Charlie Munger**

It seems obvious. Of course an asset manager's interests will be aligned with their investors'. They want their funds to generate the strongest returns possible, and so do we. However, it is not quite so simple. Most asset managers' primary goal is profits, not fund performance. These two aspects may be linked, but they are not the same. Like a rat and its tail.

The profitability of an asset manager is driven by the fees it charges and the amount of money it looks after. The second element is often the defining feature of an organisation's behaviour. Few asset management firms have significant control over the fees they charge on their funds because these tend to be set at an industry level. In a highly competitive field being an outlier on fees is an option only available to a select few. Neither can they influence the level of financial markets – if equity markets drop, so too will earnings. The main lever available to them is flow. Their attempts to maximise inflows and minimise outflows into their funds will largely determine success.

Asset managers are incentivised to attract money and keep it. To do this, they play to the predilections of fund investors. Characteristic activity includes:

- Firing underperforming fund managers.

- Heavily marketing whichever funds happen to be at the top of recent performance tables.

- Encouraging continued flows into star fund managers.

- Promoting prominent themes and launching new funds to exploit them.

Asset managers actively seek to exploit and encourage the behavioural failings that we have discussed in this book. They are incentivised to do so.

This incentive problem is particularly acute at stock market listed asset managers. Outside ownership of the business means that the pressure on senior management to meet quarterly and half-yearly earnings targets can be stark. Sell-side analysts and many shareholders are not concerned about whether an asset management firm is creating an environment that will deliver long-term success for the investors in its funds; they want to see improvements in the factors that will drive near-term share price performance – the level of money under management and profits.

As we explored earlier, this is why it is so rare to see an asset manager close a successful fund to new business even when its size stymies future return potential. The performance of incumbent investors is often sacrificed for the profit from new flows.

Conflicting time horizons

The incentive alignment problem between asset managers and fund investors is not just about profits and performance, it is about time. The time horizons of asset management executives are typically far shorter than those of the investors in their company's funds. The average tenure of a CEO is just five years. Many fund investors will have horizons that span decades. This disconnect is jarring. The incentives created for an asset management CEO will be based on company performance over a handful of years; the long-run horizons that really matter to most investors in their funds are an irrelevance. Decisions that benefit them will often be to the detriment of long-term investors.

There are of course exceptions. Stock market listed asset managers face the most severe incentive alignment problems. Smaller, privately owned businesses are not subject to the same pressures as their larger counterparts. A modestly sized asset management firm running a select group of funds is still incentivised by profits, but their time horizons can be significantly longer and they may reach a level of profitability which satisfies the owners.

It is not simply the companies and individuals within the asset management industry that create an incentive problem, it is the industry itself. It is a sprawling, bloated collection of companies with a confusing assortment of options for investors. In an efficient market, we would expect to see firms and funds possessing no investment skill fade away and fail, with the spoils being enjoyed by the most talented operators. But this doesn't happen in any meaningful sense. This is because the asset management market is deeply flawed, with echoes of how we buy and sell used cars.

Why are there so many funds and why are they so expensive?

Highly paid active fund managers aren't often associated with used cars, but there is some connection. Prior to being awarded the Nobel Memorial Prize in Economic Sciences, economist George Akerlof authored a seminal paper about the market for second-hand cars in the US. In it he argued that the market was dominated by lower quality vehicles because of a gulf in knowledge between the two sides of the transaction. In almost all cases the individual selling a car knows more about it than the buyer. He called this an 'information asymmetry'.[4]

In a situation where the seller knows more about a product than the buyer, this can be used to their advantage. While the prospective purchaser can make a general assessment of a car's qualities, they are likely to have limited understanding of its detailed history. They can't be certain if it really has had one careful owner and aren't aware that it has broken down three times in the past year. In the absence of full information, it is difficult for the buyer to differentiate between cars of contrasting quality except by judging headline factors such as appearance. This leads to a price convergence between low- and high-quality cars as buyers are unable to accurately evaluate different options. In this environment those with lower-quality vehicles are incentivised to sell, unlike those with high-quality vehicles.

This creates a market with the following characteristics:

- **Fewer high-quality vehicles:** Sellers are reluctant to part with a quality vehicle if it is priced similarly to a poor one.

- **Reduced market size:** There are fewer quality cars available.

- **Reduced average quality:** The market is likely to be dominated by inferior vehicles.

- **Reduced average willingness to pay:** The overall quality of the market is reduced.

Akelof shows that if it is difficult to assess quality and price in a market, the incentive structure can become skewed and perverse, to the detriment of customers.

A similar situation exists in the market for funds.

Finding skill in a sea of randomness

A buyer of a used car is looking for quality. What is a buyer of an actively managed fund looking for? Skill. It is only worth paying extra (more than an index fund option) if we believe that the fund manager can deliver superior returns. When surveying the market for available funds we are making judgements about relative skill.

Were the market for actively managed funds exactly like Akerlof's description of the sale of used cars, we would see an information asymmetry – asset managers would know more about the skill of their fund managers than their investors. This is not the case. The defining feature of the active management market is that neither side knows for certain that skill exists or will persist.

This is an odd situation. In the majority of purchasing decisions we make – a washing machine or TV, for example – there is a reasonable level of clarity over what the key indicators of quality are and how they might influence the product's cost. In the case of active fund management, it is far more difficult to ascertain what characteristics define skill and how they should be valued. For both buyer and seller.

If fund investors cannot confidently identify skill we tend to rely on past performance as an indicator of it. But, as we have seen, this is a terrible shorthand. Not only does it fail to differentiate between genuine talent and the random vacillations of markets; strong past performance is often a prelude to weaker returns in the future. This is akin to a situation where the more five-star reviews an apartment receives on Airbnb the more likely it is to deliver disappointing holidays to future guests.

The active management market is therefore defined by three major problems: a severe difficulty identifying skill, the mistaken use of past performance as a measure of skill and a litany of low-quality operators appearing as if they are high quality because of this uncertainty.

It creates a market with these features:

- **Too many active funds/poor average quality**

  The subjectivity around what constitutes skill and the randomness of performance (particularly over shorter time horizons) means that a vast number of low-quality/unskilled active strategies can exist, creating a bloated market. Even if we have no skill, the incentive to launch a fund is very appealing.

- **Homogeneous pricing**

  The problem of discerning between different levels of skill leads to minimal distinction between active fund costs. Active funds with no evident skill (which should cost zero – at most) are priced under the assumption that they do possess skill, while the highest quality offerings may struggle to charge a 'premium' price to the wider market because the buyer is uncertain of their true quality.

- **High average price relative to average quality**

  The entire market is priced as if skill were pervasive. On balance, there are a greater number of lower quality funds overcharging than there are higher quality funds 'undercharging'; thus, the average price for active management is skewed upward.

- **Withdrawal of highly skilled operators**

  An investor with genuine skill is likely to move away from the mass market and into (even more) rewarding fields, such as hedge funds, where they can charge significantly higher fees.

These factors combine to render the market for active management low on quality, far too big and too expensive.

So why does it survive and prosper?

Never be sold a fund

Asset managers are incentivised to keep launching active funds. If they are unsure whether any of their fund managers truly possess skill and know that performance will be noisy and random, it is rational for them to proliferate and diversify. If they take enough bets then some will pay off, generate strong performance and enable them to raise assets. They can focus their attention on marketing the 'skilful' outperformers, while struggling funds can be discarded and refreshed. There is no deliberate or malicious attempt to sell inferior products, they are simply acting rationally in an environment where both buyer and seller struggle to judge the quality of the product.

The incentive structure of the industry makes it particularly dangerous for investors to be sold a fund by an asset manager. We need to be consistently aware that the asset manager is unlikely to have a better insight about the presence of skill than we do and that they will consistently attempt to market funds that they believe will appeal to us most – those with strong past performance. They are seeking to exploit our fund-buying biases.

Fund investors frequently overpay for investment in active managers who are sold as possessing investing skill but have none. How can we stop needlessly handing undeserved money to asset managers? There is one obvious solution: paying fund managers only when they succeed in meeting their objectives.

But are performance fees really the answer?

Do performance fees work?

When we invest with an active fund manager we are only doing so because we want to outperform a low cost index fund option that will simply track the market. Given that we are attempting to buy excess returns, it seems reasonable to suggest that we should only pay when they are delivered.

Performance fees appear to solve the incentive alignment problem that plagues the fund industry. When a fund charges in this manner, the reward for the asset manager is interwoven with the results generated for their investors. What is good for one is seemingly good for the other. Yet performance fees don't remove the incentive problem, they just create a range of new ones.

Rather than performance fees fostering alignment between investor and fund manager, they produce an asymmetry of interests. The fund manager will reap profits when they generate gains, but all losses that occur will be borne by the investor. This is only attractive for one side of the relationship. This structure inevitably creates a problem of moral hazard where the fund manager is incentivised to increase the risk they take because they will not suffer the consequences of poor outcomes.

The asymmetry problem is not unique to funds charging performance fees. Flat management fees still favour the fund manager (they get paid even if they suffer severe losses), but performance fees create an extreme imbalance with huge upside for the fund manager and huge risks suffered by their investors.

Performance fees can even be earned by a fund manager even when they do not generate superior returns.

Let's take a simple example.

There is a £100m fund which charges a 1% per annum management fee and receives 20% of all outperformance versus a benchmark on an annual basis. For four years the fund delivers a return of 15% against the benchmark's 10% gain; however, in the fifth year the fund loses 15%, while the benchmark again gains 10%. How do the fund manager and investor fare in this scenario?

Cumulative excess returns against benchmark and performance fees

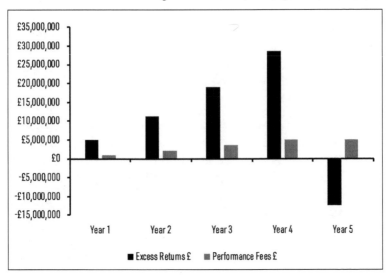

Despite four years of strong outperformance, this good work is extinguished in a terribly poor fifth year. The investor is worse off at the end of the period than if they had simply invested in an index fund. Yet this pattern of returns means that they have still paid significant performance fees. The fund manager reaped close to £5m in performance-related profits (ignoring the standard management fee) despite underperforming over the entire period.

This is not just a hypothetical example. Such situations are common. In January 2022 the *Financial Times* reported that a leading hedge fund generated £914m in firm profits in the year to March 2021. This was driven by their primary fund delivering returns of 44% in 2020. Unfortunately, they followed this with a 26% loss in 2021.[5] Over the two years this meant an underwhelming result for investors, but the hedge fund had already booked handsome profits from 2020.

There are performance fee structures whereby some form of clawback is possible, even in mutual funds, but this is an exception rather than the rule.[6] In an open-ended, daily dealing fund where the investor base is dynamic, it is close to impossible to levy performance fees in an equitable fashion. Even if there is a means of repaying underperformance this will not mitigate the inherent asymmetry.

The alignment problem of performance fees is not simply about profits, it is about time horizons. The charging structure can create a major disconnect between the investment horizon of an investor and the fund manager. If a fund has a stated investment horizon of five years, but pays performance fees on an annual basis, what date is likely to be foremost in the fund manager's thinking? If a fund manager is a month away from a large performance fee being crystallised what sort of risks are they likely to be assuming (on their investors' behalf)?

Performance fees can create short-term incentives that are likely to dominate decision making.

As well as wreaking havoc with time horizons, performance fees create perverse reference points. The charging structure typically comes with a high water mark attached; this is simply a rule that means fees can only be accrued if the value of the fund is above its previous peak level. This is to avoid a situation where fees are levied repeatedly for the same performance. While a necessary constraint, it creates incentive problems, most notably how behaviour may alter depending on where fund performance resides relative to this reference point. If a fund is languishing well beneath it after a difficult spell, then the fund manager may be motivated to embrace risk to close the gap to earn the most lucrative fees. Conversely, if above the mark, a manager might become more risk conscious as they seek to retain the profitable status of the fund.

Performance fees serve to disconnect our interests from those of the fund manager.

Handsome profits for dumb luck

The principal problem with performance fees is that they reward sheer good luck. We know that fund manager performance is heavily influenced by randomness and highly variable. This makes rewarding outcomes entirely nonsensical. Performance fees do not discern between the skilful and the fortunate investor, and will lavish gratuitous profits on those that happen to be in the right place at the right time.

It may sound an absurd contention given that outperformance above some benchmark or index fund investment is the ultimate goal of employing active investment management, but the fees levied should not be about performance in isolation. Active management fees should be paid because the fund investor believes that the underlying investment process (in the broadest sense of the term) is of sufficient quality that it materially increases the probability of delivering market outperformance over the long term. There can be no guarantees; in a system with a high degree of randomness even good decisions can lead to disappointing outcomes.

Lower flat fees not performance fees

Performance fees are not simply a flawed attempt to align the interests of clients and fund managers; they are an incredibly penal tax on investor capital. There is little justification for an asset management company taking 10–20% of an investor's outperformance. This practice is particularly punitive when a fund uses cash as its benchmark and an asset manager can enjoy staggeringly high profits simply by benefitting from the rising tide of holding risky assets.

The combination of a flat fee and a performance fee is also troubling. If an asset manager is taking a share of an investor's profits, what is the 1–2% annual management charge for? We are only paying a base fee for the prospect of outperformance; why should we be paying twice?

Performance fees are only used because the correct solution is unpalatable to many. Fees need to be flat and they need to be lower.

If performance fees serve as a masquerade for the alignment of interest between client and fund manager, is there anything that really does serve that purpose? One favourite of fund investors is co-investment. We feel more comfortable when we know that the fund manager is invested alongside us.

But should we?

Is it good news if a fund manager invests alongside us?

As fund investors we love to hear a fund manager say that they are personally invested in the strategy we are about to buy. Not only does it feel like a validation that the fund manager genuinely believes in what they are doing, it also means that they have skin in the game. They will feel our losses and gains. It matters to them.

This seems like a scenario that fosters a genuine alignment of interests, but is that true?

Although there are not reams of evidence, there are indications of a positive impact of fund managers investing in their own funds. It has been argued that fund manager ownership is the second-best predictor of future outperformance (behind fees), that there is a positive correlation between excess returns and the level of managerial ownership, and even that it leads to funds exhibiting less downside risk.[7]

If there is a performance advantage for funds where the manager is also invested, why would this be the case? It might be that they have some insight about future performance and therefore invest their monies accordingly, but given the difficulty of predicting market conditions, this seems unlikely. The more probable cause is focus and attention. Not only does the fund hold the manager's assets but it is likely to be the one upon which their remuneration is based. If they must decide how to allocate time, then this fund is likely to become a priority. In days gone by, such funds might also have received favourable trade allocations, but this is unlikely to occur in the modern regulatory environment.

Fund managers are likely to run several different funds and strategies. It is crucial for investors to understand where the manager is placing their own money. If they are investing in something else and, crucially, if they are investing in a different fund to the one which we are, why?

Investing alongside a fund manager *seems* like a simple situation where alignment of interests leads to better outcomes. Unfortunately, it is not quite that easy.

The downside of skin in the game

For a fund manager to be heavily invested in a strategy that they run is typically applauded, but from a pure investment standpoint it is imprudent. Having both your career and savings deeply entwined may show conviction but can also display negligence of the concept of prudent diversification and risk management. The most basic piece of financial advice is that it is incredibly risky to hold a significant amount of stock in the company that employs us. If something goes wrong our financial fortunes are doubly exposed – both salary and savings. This is the one situation where we seem comfortable for a fund manager to show ill-discipline and a disregard for risk.

We want a fund manager's interest to be aligned to ours, and investing alongside them does go some way to achieving that, but there is a limit. As a fund manager invests more of their net worth into their fund it will reach a tipping point where the alignment starts to wane. The more financially dependent they are on the success of the fund, the more likely they are to be focused on their own interests rather than ours. I have often heard fund managers attempt to extol their belief in their own strategy by claiming that all their liquid assets are invested in it. Do we really want a manager to be so financially reliant on the outcomes of their fund?

Even if a fund manager invests a modest portion of their wealth into a fund it is dangerous to take this as some sort of affirmation. There is a not insignificant chance that they are in a better position to bear a loss than we are. An incredibly well-remunerated fund manager taking a punt on a speculative strategy they manage – because they can easily afford the cost if it fails – is not a good guide to where we should invest a significant portion of our pension. If a fund manager's objectives and situation are different to ours, we should not assume alignment.

It is far too easy to say that investing in a fund alongside its manager creates a harmonious and beneficial alignment of interests. Context matters. While a fund manager not investing in any of their strategies is a clear warning sign, it does not follow that the more they invest the stronger the signal is for us to buy. We need to understand the behaviour and aims of the fund manager to judge how aligned we want to be.

What is the solution to the alignment problem?

There is no perfect solution to the alignment problem. The interests of asset management companies and fund managers are often and unfortunately disconnected from their investors. There are some steps the industry must take to improve the situation:

- Every fund should specify an asset under management limit at the outset and be clear about the point at which higher assets are likely to generate lower returns.

- Fees for active management should be fixed and lower to compensate investors for the odds of out/underperformance.

- Maximum fees earned by a fund should be capped to discourage unchecked asset growth and protect investors.

- Asset managers should create fee structures for funds that incentivise investors by reducing charges for long-term holders.

These recommendations will not appeal to many asset management companies because they are likely to compromise short-term profits. Such steps are, however, critical in restoring investor trust and putting their interests first.

The alignment problem within the industry is not a giant conspiracy or malevolent plot to defraud clients or make them worse off. It is not even a conscious choice. It is just the nature of the incentives within the system.

And if we want to understand behaviour, then we always need to look at the incentives.

One of the defining features of the incentive alignment problem is how it fosters rampant short-termism. Asset managers and their shareholders are obsessed with near-term performance and fund flows, which means that their behaviour tends to encourage investor myopia. This robs investors of their one true advantage – a long-term approach. I will show why this is so important in the chapter ahead.

Ten-point fund investor checklist – incentives

1. **Is the fund managed by a stock market listed asset manager?**

   An asset manager that is stock market listed is likely to be more focused on short-term flows and profitability.

2. **What does the Chief Executive of the asset manager say to shareholders?**

   The words of the Chief Executive to their shareholders will often provide a great insight into how focused they are on the long-term interests of investors in their funds, relative to shareholders. Beware talk of attempts to improve short-term performance.

3. **Does the asset manager have a history of closing funds because of size and capacity?**

   The best indication that an asset manager puts the interest of its clients first is the willingness to close funds to new investors to protect incumbent investors, preserving performance and sacrificing near-term profits.

4. **How reliant is the asset management business on a single fund or strategy?**

   The more reliant an asset manager is on a single fund, the more problematic it is for investors. It means that they are likely to continue marketing the strategy, that they are acutely vulnerable to underperformance and outflows, and are sharply focused on short-term results.

5. **What is the average tenure of senior management and how are they remunerated?**

   A high turnover in executive management and remuneration based on short-term stock price performance are not signs of a long-term investment culture.

6. **Does the fund charge performance fees?**

   The fee structure of a fund can transform the incentives of a fund manager.

7. **How are performance fees charged?**

Performance fees come in many guises and can profoundly impact fund manager behaviour. It is critical to understand the time horizon over which performance is assessed, when fees are drawn, what performance is compared to and whether there is a clawback policy.

8. **Where is the fund in its performance fee cycle?**

The behaviour of the fund manager will be heavily influenced by the performance fee cycle. Consideration should be given to where performance is relative to its high watermark, how close the fund is to crystallising a performance fee and what performance fees have been received historically.

9. **Is the fund manager invested in the fund?**

We should seek to understand how a fund manager invests, how much they invest and why. If they are invested in other funds, we must find out what they are.

10. **Does the asset manager put long-term investor interests first?**

Is there any evidence of the asset management company sacrificing near-term profits in the long-term interest of investors? Examples would include closing successful funds to new flows, imposing fee caps/limits on fund size/revenue, low staff turnover, remuneration based on long-term results and tolerance for periods of underperformance.

CHAPTER 9

A LONG TIME HORIZON IS A FUND INVESTOR'S GREATEST ADVANTAGE

O UR TIME HORIZON is the most important aspect of fund investing. As we extend it, we leverage the silent power of compounding and tip the balance towards skill and away from luck in our investment decisions. As we shorten it, we leave ourselves beholden to the ravages and frustrations of unpredictability, while incurring a catalogue of both visible and hidden costs.

In this chapter I show why most investor time horizons are too short to warrant owning active funds. I also explain how we can lengthen our time horizons by stopping the search for the perfect fund and avoiding decisions during periods of panic. I close by explaining why playing Russian roulette alone is a bad idea and when adopting a long-term approach increases the risks we face.

But first I look at why active fund investors would have fired the best investor of our lifetime on multiple occasions.

When would we fire Warren Buffett?

Warren Buffett is undoubtedly the most famous active investor of his generation, and one of the most successful. Between 1965 and 2021 his company, Berkshire Hathaway, produced a compounded annual return of 20.1%, compared to 10.5% for the S&P 500. This translates into a gain over the period of a staggering 3,641,613% versus (just) 30,209% for the S&P 500.[1]

These astronomical results represent an astonishing achievement and beg the question – if we had been invested with Buffett through this period, at what point would we have fired him?

Because we would almost certainly have done so.

Most investors have limited tolerance for underperformance. Even if we have investment objectives that stretch out to 30 or 40 years, we still care greatly about what is happening in the short term. Two or three years of sub-par results tends to be the limit of acceptability before we move on to a new fund with a better recent track record.[2]

This is a fatal flaw in how we invest in active funds. It is so profound that, if we cannot overcome it, we should not even consider investing with active fund managers.

A 2019 article by UBS looked at the historic performance of Berkshire Hathaway from 1988 onwards.[3] It explained how the frequency of outperformance was intrinsically related to the time horizon involved. The longer the time period, the greater the incidence of outperformance.

Over short spells of days, weeks and months the relative results were little more than a coin toss – not substantially different to a 50/50 chance. Yet when this was extended to ten years, Berkshire Hathaway outperformed on close to 90% of occasions.

Time horizons change everything.

The typical period of patience active fund investors have for underperformance before they throw in the towel and sell is three years. Berkshire's success rate here was close to 60%. This means that in over 40% of observed three-year periods, Buffett trailed the market. We would have fired him and fired him regularly.

If our preferred time horizon for assessing fund performance means that we fire one of the greatest proponents of the art, then it must be wrong.

Why do time horizons matter so much?

Because the shorter our timespan the more beholden our results are to chance; if we lengthen it then skill can have a greater impact.

The profits and dividends of a company will have no influence on what a share price does tomorrow, but will mean a great deal over the next decade. If our time horizon is short then our investment in an active fund is nothing more than a roll of the dice, and an expensive one at that.

But this is not a story about Warren Buffett; it is about all active funds.

In a 2021 study, Vanguard looked at a group of 1,173 actively managed US domiciled funds that had delivered outperformance over a 25-year period. They found that near 100% of the funds had, at some point, experienced underperformance relative to their peer group over one, three and five years.[4]

Even if we had managed to identify an active fund with the ability to deliver excess returns, we almost certainly would have sold it during an inevitable spell of poor performance.

This phenomenon starkly shows the second element of the twin challenges of selecting an active fund. We don't just need to be able to identify a talented manager or strategy, we need to stick with them.

Before even considering an investment in an active fund there are two critical principles to consider:

1. If we cannot bear sustained periods of underperformance relative to a market cap index then we should not own active funds.

2. If we do not have a long time horizon (ten years or more) then we should not own active funds.

Does the requirement for having a long-term approach mean that we must persist with active funds no matter what? Absolutely not, there are countless reasons why we might lose confidence in an active manager, many of which are covered in this book. The critical point is that if we are to even contemplate investing in active funds we must be willing to hold for the long term. It is a necessary but not sufficient condition for success.

But do we really know what our time horizon is?

What is our true investment time horizon?

Understanding our time horizon is far more difficult than it seems. It is easy to think of it as merely a start and end point, but it is far more than that. To recognise our true time horizon, we need to consider three elements: our objective, our interactions and our activity.

Our objective

This seems like the easy part. We can gauge our time horizon by simply understanding the main goal of our investment. If it is for our pension, the aim might be to reach retirement in 30 years. If we are a fund manager, it might be to grow the fund over the five years stated in its prospectus. If we are taking a punt on a stock it might be a month.

Unfortunately, it is not quite so simple.

There can be a sharp disconnect between our explicit and implicit investment objectives. Let's take the fund manager example. Their formal fund objective states a time horizon of five years, but their remuneration is based on returns over one year. They have also been going through a difficult period of performance, and both their manager and clients are focused on the next quarter's results.

Over what time horizon are they now making decisions?

Even in the case of our personal pension, the 30-year goal creates a theoretical time horizon but not necessarily a practical one. If we fill our pension with the latest flavour of the month thematic funds, we are not thinking about three decades hence; we are trying to turn a healthy profit over the next year.

Our ability to assume more investment risk when we have a long-term investment objective can easily be used as a licence to make a succession of ill-judged, shorter-term decisions – assuming exactly the wrong sort of risks.

The time horizon that stems from our investment objectives is about the specific incentives and pressures driving our decision. We need to define our major motivating factors.

Our interactions

Another critical aspect of our time horizon is the way in which we interact with our investments. How frequently do we check performance? How regularly do we review our decision? We can think of our time horizon as a beginning and end punctuated with a mini-horizon whenever we interact. Each time we do so we are generating a decision point – a situation where we will consciously or sub-consciously be making a judgement about whether to persist. Every interaction we have with our investments is creating the potential for us to obstruct the power of time.

Whenever we make changes to our investments it is because we think we are wrong about something. There is a better stock, a better fund, a better opportunity, a better time. Irrespective of how good our decisions are, the market will persistently lure us away from charting a sensible course. The more we engage, the more likely we are to succumb to its siren song.

Minimising interactions is probably the sternest challenge faced by investors. Rather than being viewed as behaviourally prudent, restricting the amount we check our funds is more likely to be considered negligent. This is the curse of professional investors who are required to persistently evaluate and act, irrespective of whether it is likely to be beneficial.

It is easy to think that because markets and economies are

ever changing, our investments should change too. This is absolutely the wrong conclusion.

There is an action bias inherent in fund investing which is similar to penalty kicks in professional football; here the goalkeeper tends to dive left or right, despite the optimal strategy being simply to stand still.[5] If the penalty taker scores and we fail to move, it looks far worse than if the opposing player scores but at least we dived. If we don't move, then we are not trying. The same applies to investing; while doing nothing is often the superior approach, there is a stigma attached. Hence, we end up trying to fix short-term perceptions while incurring long-term costs.

Restricting interactions with our investments is not about making one decision and then closing our eyes and ears; neither does it mean failing to review and reassess the choices we have made. It is simply about understanding the behavioural reality that the more we interact, the shorter our time horizons are likely to become. We need to engage in a measured and deliberate fashion over time periods that matter to us.

Our activity

Frequent interaction with our investments raises the probability of increased trading and turnover, but it is not a certainty. The final element to consider is our activity. We can only act if we are able to. Worrying about quarterly performance or checking our investments every day is irrelevant if it is impossible or difficult for us to trade. Our time horizon is shaped by our ability to act. If we are locked into an investment for ten years, then that is our time horizon (the real illiquidity premium!)

Limiting our activity and interactions is crucial to adopting a long-term approach, but our attempts to do so are being increasingly hindered by improving technology.

Technological innovation has meant that as investors we now have more transparency and control over our funds than ever before. This appears to be an indisputable benefit providing protection and choice. There is, however, a major downside. The more freedom we have in our investment decision making, the more opportunity there is for us to make mistakes.

The growth and availability of financial news allied to the ability for us to monitor and trade our investments on a second-by-second basis is a toxic combination, one that leads to constant monitoring, increased risk aversion and damaging overtrading. Enhanced technology not only provides us with the stimulus to act but also the means to do it. Improvements in technology have made fund investing for the long term harder and more unlikely.

If our horizons are short then having a constant option to quit or change course is invaluable. If we are long-term investors then it is an impediment. Our ability to act can frame and influence our time horizon. Better technology has made it more difficult to be a successful fund investor.

Technology is a facilitator for some of fund investors' damaging short-term behaviours, but it alone does not cause them. A primary driver of our inability to stick with an investment is the belief that there is always a better fund that we could be invested in.

Our drive to find the best is inevitably leading to worse outcomes.

When should we stop looking for the best fund?

Decision-making theory suggests that the optimal approach to a choice is to assess all available options and then select the best possible. This is, somewhat obtusely, called maximising our utility.

This model is an example of a robust concept that fails as soon as it encounters the real world.

A major critique of this approach came in the 1950s, when economist Herbert Simon suggested that rather than attempt to make the optimal choice, cognitive and environmental limitations mean that we often 'satisfice'. We make a choice when we discover an option that is 'good enough' and meets some minimum threshold criteria that we might hold.[6]

The contrast between satisficing and utility-maximising behaviour is crucial when we consider our fund investment decision making. Our natural reaction is to assume that we should be maximisers and exhaustively seek the best possible option, and it is hard to accept something simply being 'good enough'.

But should this really be the case?

No.

For fund investors attempts to maximise are not only impossible, but the fruitless and constant search for the best option can lead to very poor outcomes and dramatically cut short our intended time horizons.

There are several features about fund investments that make maximising behaviour particularly problematic.

- **Too many options**

  Maximisation may prove effective if there is a narrow and well-defined set of options, but in investment it is impossible to perform an exhaustive search across all available choices. There are over 100,000 open-ended funds registered globally. The opportunity set is enormous and fluid, and any attempt to ensure that we have selected the best will be perpetual and unproductive.

- **Vague criteria**

  Successful maximisation is also reliant on there being known and objective quality criteria – is it possible to easily differentiate between different options based on the most important factors? In fund investment it is incredibly difficult to confidently isolate these criteria and distinguish between distinct choices. This is very different to making a choice on what phone to buy or which hotel to stay in; for these choices the criteria are largely known and easily comparable.

- **Wrong criteria**

  Setting criteria when deciding is only useful when we know what factors are meaningful. In fund investing we know that our objective will be performance related (to match or beat an index, typically) but we are not entirely certain what criteria matter or how much. Even more troubling is our tendency, when investing in active funds, to use the wrong criteria: past performance.

- **Shifting criteria**

  In addition to past performance being the most frequently used but damaging criteria for fund selection, it also suffers from a lack of stability. Not only is it a weak metric for maximisation at any single point in time, but it is also changeable. The fluctuating performance of funds means that if we rely on past performance to compare options, we will be forever switching between them.

- **Simple switching**

  One of the most problematic features of attempting to maximise in a fund context is the ability to switch between options in a relatively 'frictionless' and simple fashion. While the switching costs may be reasonably low, the total cost of lurching between different funds can be exorbitant.

The attempt to maximise in fund investment decision making is highly problematic yet unfortunately common. As fund investors we are always comparing how our fund ranks compared to others and looking enviously at those that are outperforming. We know that fund outperformance is not persistent even if a manager possesses skill; thus, in seeking to maximise, we are doomed to be short term in our thinking.

Maximisation is another of the many investment behaviours that 'feels' conceptually right – of course we should be seeking a superior alternative – but has severely deleterious consequences. In addition to the problems of maximisation specific to investment decision making, it has been argued that there are other negative ramifications.

Research suggests that individuals who maximise are likely to suffer lower optimism, life satisfaction and self-esteem.[7] Psychologist Barry Schwartz also notes that as the range of options expands, our threshold for an acceptable outcome becomes too high and we are more likely to blame ourselves for disappointing results rather than circumstance or environment. There are so many good funds available, why couldn't we pick one?[8]

If we are always seeking the absolute best outcome among a multitude of choices, discontent will follow as there is likely to be consistent regret from failing to select the best.[9] The variability of performance allied to the sheer range of options in fund investing means that there will always be new shiny objects to attract us. We will never invest in a fund that is consistently top of the performance tables, nor should we try.

Attempting to maximise our fund decision making simply leads to value destruction as we chase yesterday's winners, trade too frequently and live in constant regret that the funds we don't own are performing better than those we do. Instead of this, we should be content to satisfice. Find funds that are good enough, founded on sound investment principles and suited to our objectives.

Then stick with them for the long term.

Unfortunately, even if we do this, there is another obstacle that prevents us from adopting a long-term approach. One that is even more pernicious than our constant drive to find a better fund. One that can cut our horizons from decades to minutes.

Panic.

When is the worst time to make a fund investment decision?

Panic is an overwhelming feeling of fear that can dictate our decision making. It typically begins with a significant and sudden change in circumstance. The widespread outbreak of Covid-19 in 2020 provided numerous examples of decisions that were seemingly fuelled by stress and uncertainty; from the bizarre stockpiling of toilet paper to the unprecedented size and speed of declines in equity and credit markets.

Panic results in a dramatic contraction in our time horizon.

Amid panic our concern becomes singularly focused on what is happening right at that moment. We are gripped by the fears of today and abandon any thought of the future. While in certain situations in life this can be considered an effective adaptation, for meeting our long-term investment objectives such myopia can be irreparably damaging. The causes of panic are varied, but there are common threads:

- **Scarcity**

  Panic decisions are often the result of a current or future scarcity of a good or service. The case of toilet paper hoarding in the UK during the Covid-19 pandemic is an issue driven by self-perpetuating scarcity – where the very scarcity is caused by other people's perception of it. This type of panic can persist even when nobody can remember its initial causes. It feeds on itself.

  While the scarcity issue is obvious when it comes to the panic purchases of household goods, it is also evident in financial markets. Although a fund may not be scarce, features of it may be; for example, the ability to transact in a fund at a certain price, or any price. An assumed or real limit on the ability to sell can induce panic – like the shout of "fire" in a packed theatre, we fear that the exit may not be available to us all. Issues with a fund's liquidity are often ignored until a period of panic arrives.

- **Other people**

  Panic buying and selling is always about how we react to the behaviour of others (and how they react to us). This comes in several guises:

  - **The 'wisdom' of crowds:** Panic can be caused by the assumption that there is information in the behaviour of others, and the greater the number of people engaging in certain activities the more we believe that they possess knowledge that we do not. The problem is that crowd wisdom tends to arise in situations when there is a level of diversity of thought and an independence in how people in the crowd have reached a view. When panic buying or selling occurs, the reverse is true. The behaviour of the group is a result of individuals reacting to the same, very narrow set of information, or simply following others. The wisdom of crowds swiftly becomes the madness.

- **Thresholds:** In a related fashion, sometimes we simply act because other people are, even when we are not aware of what is driving the initial behaviour. Sociologist Mark Granovetter described a threshold model where a decision made by an individual to engage in a riot is led simply by how many other people are doing it. Each individual will have a different threshold for engaging in 'mob' behaviour, which is the point at which "the perceived benefits to the individual of doing the thing in question, exceed the perceived costs."[10]

- **Failing conventionally:** The notion that our propensity to join mass group behaviour is related to some form of cost/benefit threshold is intertwined with our preference for 'failing conventionally', which is a huge influence on the behaviour of professional fund investors. The management of career risk and the desire to protect our reputation or business means that the behaviour of others matters profoundly, irrespective of whether we agree with or understand it. Even if our behaviour is extremely irrational from any fundamental investment perspective, it can be supremely rational for us as individuals. We are less likely to lose our job doing what everybody else is. If we are going to be wrong, don't be wrong alone.

- **Removing worry**

As panic is a result of fear and anxiety, the actions that come as a consequence are typically carried out in an effort to relieve it. Our decision making becomes centred on a single goal: removing worry. The greater the uncertainty and the less control we feel we have, the sharper the urgency for us to act. Panic buying and selling occurs when the cause of the worry is shared by many people, which results in numerous individuals taking similar actions. As with the other primary causes of panic, these actions become self-reinforcing. The desire of others to reduce their own worry serves to create and increase fear in others.

What was the easy way for investors to mitigate the fear and uncertainty around the financial and economic impact of Covid-19 in March 2020? To sell risky assets and hold cash.

Although it may have been a damaging long-term decision, this was outweighed by the palpable short-term relief. Even with the mystifying toilet paper hoarding there were similar factors at play; once we have filled the garage with 600 rolls, we no longer expend energy worrying about not having enough.

- **Emotional decision making**

  Our attitude towards a given risk is heavily influenced by its emotional salience. How we perceive both the likelihood and magnitude of a threat can be dominated by its prominence (or availability) and how it makes us feel. As Cass Sunstein discusses in his work on probability neglect, if something provokes a strong emotional reaction then we tend to disregard how likely that risk is to occur and focus on its potential impact (usually the worst-case scenario).[11] When decisions are made in a state of panic, risk becomes about how we feel, not how we think.

There is an irony inherent to the travails of investing in times of panic. It makes us incredibly short term in our thinking, but it is the best time to be a long-term investor. Long-term returns following periods of crisis tend to be higher (because valuations become cheaper) and they are also more predictable. The patterns of performance across and within asset classes are more consistent through and following a crisis.[12]

Panic buying and selling represents the very worst of our investment behaviours; it is emotion-laden, focused on the short term and driven by the behaviour of other people. While it can have incredibly harmful long-term consequences for investors, it offers the often irresistible allure of making us feel better and worry less, immediately.

The ability to prepare for and manage situations where we are gripped by panic can improve our prospects of being genuinely long-term fund investors and obtaining all the benefits that brings. Yet a long-term approach is not a guarantee of success. There are even situations where the longer our time horizon, the greater the risks.

Is a long time horizon always a good thing?

A long-term approach to fund investing is the one great advantage freely available to us all. It transforms the odds of us meeting our objectives. Yet taking such an approach is not always a good idea. There are situations where extending our time horizon can substantially increase the risk of bad outcomes. To understand why, let's play Russian roulette.

We have a gun with the capacity to hold six bullets, but with only one bullet in the chamber. We use it for a game of Russian roulette with a group of 19 other people. Each of us takes one turn in spinning the chamber, holding the gun to our temple and pulling the trigger. If we are successful we win £1m; if not, well, then we die. While this may not be an appealing proposition, our chance of death is relatively low (17%), and potential for becoming a millionaire high (83%).

This is a far more attractive option than an alternative version of the game where instead of playing with a group, we play on our own. In this instance there are still 20 turns but each time the gun is directed at our head.

Our chances of success in this instance are not so favourable.

If we make a poor decision where there is a risk of catastrophic losses, a long time horizon works against us. It materially increases our risk of bad outcomes.

Imagine that we decide not to buy home insurance. We have had a policy for ten years and never had to make a claim. Also, we know that insurance companies make a profit from selling it, so we must be making a loss. Paying the premiums seems like a waste of money.

Here we have made a bad decision, which becomes worse with each day that goes by. One day without home insurance is an entirely different proposition to ten years without it.

Why does this matter to fund investors?

If we invest in funds that carry the potential for extreme, permanent losses, then – contrary to most aspects of investment – extending our time horizon increases the level of risk we face. Each day we maintain our holding is akin to pulling the trigger once again in the game of Russian roulette.

The longer we were invested in Bernie Madoff's fraudulent funds, the greater the chance that we were holders the moment the swindle was discovered.

Whenever we concentrate our wealth in something with the potential for severe and permanent losses – such as an individual stock, a poorly diversified fund, an individual theme or a complex, leveraged hedge fund – then we invert a key principle of sound investing. A longer time horizon works against us; it increases the probability of disaster.

Of course, we all face the prospect of sharp losses. An investor with a prudently diversified portfolio of equity funds and a 40-year time horizon will experience multiple bear markets where their wealth will be temporarily savaged. The difference is that these are unlikely to be permanent. They are recoverable. Time works in our favour here; it is when the potential losses are irretrievable that it becomes our enemy.

We cannot hope to understand the return and risk prospects of our investments without first considering time.

Why is time so important?

It is so easy to neglect time, yet it is the first thing we should consider when making any fund investment decision. If we can adopt a genuinely long-term approach – more than ten years – then we can harness the power of compounding and dull the often overwhelming impact of superfluous noise. The positive impact of time, if we manage our behaviour prudently, will overwhelm everything else we do as investors. There is no greater investment edge.

A long time horizon is no panacea. It does not turn a bad decision into a good one, but a short-term approach will almost inevitably turn our good decisions into bad ones.

Frustratingly, it is astonishingly difficult to use time to our advantage. As fund investors we must experience and withstand the vagaries of performance and continually question whether we have invested with the right manager or the best asset classes. The temptation to cut our time horizons by persistently reacting to noise and the incessant stream of news by changing our investments is often irresistible. Over the long term we will be frequently tested by periods of stress and uncertainty.

The higher returns available for a long-term approach only exist because it is difficult to do. Not difficult technically – it doesn't require sophistication or science – but it requires us to understand our behaviour and manage it.

To be a long-term investor takes a huge amount of effort to do less.

Adopting the mindset of a long-term investor not only improves the chances of meeting our objectives but also affords us space to consider the broader impact our investment decisions might have. This wider perspective is the critical underpinning to the growth of ESG investing, which has become the dominant theme in the asset management industry in recent years. The next chapter uncovers what it really means.

Ten-point fund investor checklist – long-term investing

I. **How long could we persevere with an underperforming fund?**

    If two to three years of underperformance is sufficient to persuade us to fire a manager, we should be buying only index funds.

2. **Are we combining different types of active fund?**

    The best protection against short-term, performance-driven thinking in fund investing is combining different types of managers with distinct approaches and styles. When one is undergoing a difficult spell of performance another might be enjoying a more fruitful period.

3. **What is our ultimate investment time horizon?**

    Our correct time horizon is our ultimate objective – the reason we are saving and investing.

4. **What time horizons do we actually care about?**

    The more realistic time horizon is the one that drives our behaviour.

5. **How often are we trading?**

    Any trading should be consistent with our long-term objective.

6. **How frequently are we looking for new funds?**

    Constantly searching for new funds is likely to result in high turnover and value-destructive performance chasing. To be a long-term investor we must create an approach that reduces our interactions and activity.

7. **What are the key criteria for assessing new funds?**

    These must include more than past performance.

8. **Are we prepared for poor performance from our funds during periods of market stress?**

    To deal with periods of market stress we must prepare for them. If we are investing in equity funds then losses of at least 30% are inevitable over a market cycle. If we do not accept this we will make bad decisions when the time arrives.

9. **Do we have a plan for stressed markets?**

Not only should we be aware of the reality of drawdowns and losses, we should plan for them. We never know what will cause them, but we know they will occur. We must have a positive plan that is consistent with our long-term goals.

10. **Do we hold funds with the risk of extreme permanent losses?**

Long-term investing is only a bad idea if we take unnecessary risks in concentrated or complex funds.

CHAPTER 10

SEEING BEYOND THE MYTHS AND MARKETING OF ESG INVESTING

I N RECENT YEARS ESG (Environmental, Social and Governance) investing has come to dominate the asset management landscape. The movement is fuelled by the idea that businesses have responsibilities that stretch beyond generating profits for their shareholders. They have a duty to consider a far broader group of stakeholders, from employees to wider society to the planet.

ESG investing seeks to assess businesses across a huge range of areas from biodiversity and climate change (Environment), to modern slavery and working conditions (Social), and board diversity and pay (Governance). It asks investors to consider these factors when allocating capital and to reward the best companies, while holding less exposure to, or entirely excluding, the worst actors. The movement has been widely embraced not only by investors but also by politicians and regulators.[1]

Asset managers have also been keen to join the party. As they strive to protect declining active management revenues many, who have never previously mentioned sustainability or ESG, now claim to be lifelong advocates with ESG 'in their DNA'.

Although the rise of ESG investing should be a positive for fund investors, it has made our lives more difficult. As asset managers strive for credibility in this field there has been an explosion of metrics, definitions and new or rebranded funds. It has become difficult to tell what is meaningful and what is marketing spin.

Through this chapter I seek to disentangle sense from sales and provide a framework for thinking about the key factors to incorporate when making ESG fund choices. I consider whether excluding companies whose activities we disagree with really achieves anything, if ESG is just another marketing angle for asset managers, and if ESG investing is likely to lead to better performance. I close by arguing that the rise of ESG investing means thinking about the funds we own generating an entirely different type of return – one that we are unlikely to notice.

But first I look at the dilemma faced by shareholders in the age of ESG investing.

Should oil companies be buying wind farms?

The oil production company BP does not have a fantastic environmental pedigree. It paid the largest environmental fine in US history for the 2010 Deepwater Horizon oil spill and a judge labelled their actions "grossly negligent."[2] The Climate Accountability Institute identified it as one of the largest shareholder-owned carbon dioxide emitters.[3]

Given that the company is involved in the extraction and burning of fossil fuels these characteristics are perhaps unremarkable. What is more surprising is the management of BP's change of strategy in 2020. They plan to be investing $5bn per year in renewable energy by 2030, cutting oil and gas production by over 40%, and have committed to reducing their net carbon emissions to zero by 2050.[4]

For a major oil company this shift in strategy is a bold reflection of growing shareholder desire for companies to account for and address the costs that their activities bring to bear on society – so-called externalities. Yet for many their actions are too little, too late. Fossil fuel production needs to be slashed during the 2020s if there is any hope of limiting global temperature increases to the well below 2 degrees Celsius levels defined in the Paris Agreement and subsequently enhanced in Glasgow at COP26.[5]

It can also be argued that BP is using sleight of hand to overstate their climate change credentials. Their ambition to reduce carbon emissions to zero is based only on their production and operations activity, not the products they sell. This is akin to a tobacco company stating that they are not responsible for the carcinogenic nature of the cigarettes they make because somebody else smokes them.

It is, however, hypocritical for most of us to be sanctimonious about the activities of BP as we work on our computers, sit in a centrally heated house, and drive our petrol cars, but the attempted shift in approach of the business strikes at the heart of how we view ESG investing.

What do shareholders want?

At its core the transition towards ESG investing is driven by the disconnect between the attempt of companies to maximise returns to shareholders and the impact their activities have on other stakeholders and wider society. The doctrine of shareholder value maximisation stems from Milton Friedman and his assertion that the "social responsibility of business is to increase its profits."[6] Although there is more nuance to Friedman's view than his 1970 statement suggests, it is hard to dispute the notion that his philosophy has aptly defined the behaviour of most companies and shareholders in recent decades.

Listed companies have an obligation to their owners – that is, their shareholders. This commitment is typically viewed as generating the highest possible returns on capital for their business activities and producing a rising stream of profits. The same is true for fund investors. We desire the strongest performance from the investments made by the fund manager we select. Until recently these ideas would have been uncontroversial and rarely disputed, but is this still the case?

Has the entire notion of shareholder value maximisation changed?

In a 2021 interview with the *Financial Times*, Patrick Pouyanne, the

CEO of French oil and gas company Total, stated that the flow of capital into the renewable energy sector had led to extreme valuations for assets in the area.[7] Such conditions may create the prospect of low future returns on capital invested in the clean energy industry, which creates a quandary for the major oil companies. Should they invest in potentially expensive assets which are aligned to ESG objectives, or seek to boost the returns of their traditional fossil fuels business?

This is a critical question for shareholders and investors to answer. Let's take an example.

A large oil company is considering investing in a sizeable offshore windfarm project. The investment would help the business transition away from fossil fuels, but the flood of capital into renewable energy projects means that the expected returns from the windfarms are low in all but the most optimistic scenarios. Significantly lower than the returns that they enjoy on their existing business.

Should they make the investment?

From Friedman's perspective the answer is clearly no, companies should not be making decisions that diminish the value of a business, and, if they do, they are failing to act in the best interests of their shareholders. But investors seem to be increasingly supportive of this type of activity. Indeed BP would not have embarked on its transformation plan if it had not been demanded. Why are investors encouraging developments that may reduce the returns they make? There are four potential explanations:

1. They do not see such projects as low return and believe they are a superior use of capital even from a classical, shareholder profit maximisation perspective.

2. The strong flows into stocks with positive ESG stories will boost the share price, irrespective of whether it is profitable.

3. They are willing to accept lower returns because of the greater stakeholder good delivered by the move to renewable energy. In essence, the argument here is that shareholder returns are a much broader concept than the dividends we receive from an investment.

4. Over the very long run, fossil fuel activities will be obsolete, whereas returns from renewable energy will persist. If you stretch your time horizon into the distance, the latter activity may be more valuable.

Different investors will have different perspectives on the scenario presented, but to navigate the field of ESG investing as it develops we must have a clear opinion on it. It is naïve to believe that positive ESG investing actions immediately and automatically lead to better returns. Instead, we must consider what we want to achieve from our investments outside of the narrow lens of investment performance, and whether we are willing to sacrifice returns to achieve it.

This is crucial for fund investors. ESG investing in its various guises will be the most important theme in asset management during the 2020s, and even if we are ambivalent we cannot ignore its implications. Specialist sustainability and impact funds will become commonplace and all active managers will incorporate ESG factors (or at least claim they do).

Index funds will not be immune to this movement. Bespoke 'ESG' index funds will compete with traditional market cap versions and passive fund providers will seek to differentiate themselves by wielding the huge influence they have as major shareholders to effect positive change.

Understanding exactly what we want to achieve from our investments will become a little more complicated.

The simplest step that fund investors can take along the path of ESG-friendly investing is to stop owning certain companies and industries. If we are unhappy with the impact of BP on the environment, then surely not buying it is the solution?

Does excluding certain types of company really make a difference?

Ethical funds were the somewhat-niche forerunner to ESG investing. Typically, they were focused on exclusions; their investable universe was shorn of stocks that were involved in controversial business practices such as animal testing, tobacco, or gambling. These were value-based judgements rather than informed by financial considerations. They appealed to investors who were not comfortable holding exposure to particular activities.

ESG investing is a far broader endeavour than the traditional ethical fund approach. It seeks to actively identify good actors rather than just cut out the bad. Exclusions, however, remain an important feature.

In 2021, as part of its drive towards a more sustainable investment approach, the £3.5bn Cambridge University endowment committed to divest from fossil fuels entirely by 2030.[8] This followed a prolonged bout of severe student protest and pressure. Scores of other university investment funds had already made divestment pledges, as had a broad range of other institutions including the Church of England.[9] Intuitively, this seems like a rational and considered approach – the best way to prevent the impending climate crisis is to stop investing in and funding some of the worst polluting companies.

Does this really work?

Bill Gates doesn't think so. The Microsoft founder and climate philanthropist argued that divestment has likely had no impact on reducing emissions. Instead he recommends investing in companies involved in innovation and technological change as far more efficacious.[10]

Divestment can be ineffective because it does not change anything for the company that we have excluded. When we divest, somebody else buys the shares which we relinquish. They may have very different objectives and principles to those which we hold. Our divestment means we have no voice in how the company is run in the future or the strategic decisions it takes. Our funds may look better from an ESG perspective, but it is possible that people and the planet are worse off.

Take BP, widespread divestment might mean that its share price falls and cost of capital increases, but this would likely result in other more willing investors stepping in and enjoying higher returns. The new and remaining shareholders might focus on near-term profits rather than ESG issues, encouraging BP to abandon its move towards renewable energy and instead to maximise short-term profits from increased extraction of fossil fuels.

That is not to say divestment is a bad idea. It is perfectly reasonable from a personal values perspective to have certain industries or companies in which we are uncomfortable owning a stake. We may also be keen to avoid industries that we believe are in decline because of their environmental or social risks. We should not, however, imagine that simply by not holding a business we are removing the problem. Nor should we lightly discard our ability to engage with companies.

The rules of engagement

When investors relinquish their holdings in a company, they also part with any ability to influence their future activities through engagement. Engagement is the process by which equity owners and lenders to a business can use their position to influence corporate decision making. This can take the form of private discussions with senior management, public statements and voting at annual general meetings. As ESG investing has flourished, engagement has become a crucial means for asset managers to prove their credentials on environmental, social and governance issues.

For fund investors engagement is vital. Asset managers are investing money on our behalf; by aggregating the assets of many, they wield the power to shape the corporate landscape. We should only invest if we are comfortable that they are using our money in a responsible way. Are they holding management to account for the issues that matter to us?

It is easy to be dismissive of the power of engagement and see it as an ineffectual activity that is simply used as an excuse for not divesting from companies involved in controversial practices. But it can really make a difference. The best example of this is the Climate Action 100+ group.

Formed in the wake of the 2015 Paris Agreement to limit global temperatures to well below 2 degrees above pre-industrial levels, Climate Action 100+ is a collaboration between some of the world's most prominent investors. Its aim is to engage with the largest greenhouse gas emitters to ensure that they report their environmental impact in a transparent fashion and commit to reducing emissions.

The group has over 615 signatory investors responsible for over $65trn in assets. Their focus is on 167 companies, responsible for over 80% of industrial emissions.[11] Given the scale of assets, this form of collective engagement can be incredibly influential. It is highly unlikely that a company like BP would have embarked on their new sustainability strategy without pressure from shareholder and investor groups such as Climate Action 100+.

Engagement can function on two levels. Investors can encourage or force individual companies to alter their behaviour regarding issues such as executive remuneration or a planned merger. These engagements can be impactful but are idiosyncratic. More meaningful is where the majority of shareholders and investors coalesce around a view about what is acceptable and desired corporate behaviour. The weight of this type of movement can be irresistible for most companies and promote genuine change.

This is no panacea. It is far too easy for asset managers to employ virtue-signalling behaviour without taking any meaningful actions. Engagement can also be agonisingly slow and piecemeal in nature. It has taken years for index fund giants such as Vanguard and BlackRock to engage more meaningfully on critical ESG issues.[12] Also, positive engagement on ESG topics does not necessarily come with better future returns.

Fund investors need to take engagement seriously and they should be willing to hold asset managers to account for how they wield the influence they hold. We must always ask how a fund manager engages with investee companies and why. It might be that they engage solely when they believe it may impact financial returns, not regarding purely ESG-related improvements. We should seek to understand the factors that drive their engagement behaviour.

One of the major challenges of engagement is knowing which concerns fund managers should engage on. ESG encompasses such a huge range of issues, how do we decide what is important?

Which ESG issues really matter?

ESG investing is dominated by the issue of climate change, which is understandable given the profound threat it poses to humanity. It is, however, only one element of ESG. MSCI – one of the leading ESG ratings providers – identifies 35 key issues encompassing areas such as carbon emissions, water stress, labour management and business ethics.[13]

All businesses face and pose different risks. Comparing them against each other – which is a central tenet of ESG investing – is incredibly difficult. If a company has excellent labour management but their activities are a threat to biodiversity, are they a good company from an ESG perspective? What matters more? If a company shuts down a thermal coal mine, which leads to thousands of job losses in a poverty-stricken area, is that a positive or negative development?

There are no simple answers to any of these questions. The importance of different issues will depend on how they are being judged. It might be about their financial impact on the company in question or about the values that we hold. The challenge becomes even more exacting when we begin to compare companies operating in different sectors. Is it possible to reasonably compare the ESG qualities of a gold mining company and a social media business?

There are two extreme and opposed approaches that can be taken when faced with the complex realities of ESG investing. We can say it is so difficult, incoherent and inconsistent as to render it a pointless activity. Alternatively, we can argue that some areas and issues are just more important than others; there is a right way to invest sustainably, and a wrong way. Both perspectives are flawed.

To capture the potential benefits of ESG investing and its ability to improve business practices and aid society and the planet, we need to accept its inconsistencies. That each rating agency and asset manager has a different perspective of what makes good ESG practice is frustrating but inevitable. The field is nascent and highly subjective; there is no right answer. Simply because the endeavour is imperfect does not mean it cannot do a great deal of good. The general principles of ESG investing are consistent and encourage improved behaviour from companies. The nuances should be of less importance.

Fund investors should take one of two approaches: either invest in funds where we are comfortable that the philosophy regarding ESG investing is considered and robust, or – for those with more strident views – identify funds where the values and approach align with our own.

Despite its imperfections, the movement towards ESG investing should prove a net positive for people and the planet. There is one risk that could derail it, however: the involvement of asset managers.

Is ESG investing just an asset management marketing ploy?

A major problem for ESG investing is the motives of the asset management industry, which has embraced the movement with staggering alacrity. The damascene conversion of asset managers has coincided with sustained and sizeable outflows from actively managed funds and declining profitability. How can active asset managers stem the tide of monies away from them and into index funds and maintain high margins? By selling the ESG story.

If asset managers had simply said that they have now begun to incorporate ESG factors into their investment process because of increasing client demand, this would have been honest and credible. This is not the approach many have adopted. Instead, they have rewritten history, with many making the fatuous claim that ESG investing is "in their DNA." Unfortunately, they forgot to mention it until recently. This is a brazen sales tactic and one so obviously spurious that it just fosters investor distrust of the entire enterprise.

In a parallel universe where performance of ESG-tilted funds had been poor for a decade and there was little prospect of it attracting investor flows, it is a sad but inalienable truth that the same asset managers would have a different genetic makeup – one where factors that are now paramount are not quite so prominent. As we have already learned, incentives matter.

It is a grim irony that the movement towards better ESG investment practices – which involves broadening the narrow concept of shareholder value maximisation – has been driven by many asset managers attempting to maximise shareholder value.

What's measured is what matters

Does it really matter why asset managers have so readily embraced ESG investing? Unfortunately, it does. For ESG investing to have meaningful long-term benefits there needs to be a lasting commitment to it. It cannot be a fleeting engagement which ends as soon as performance deteriorates.

Asset managers are currently involved in a competition to prove their ESG mettle. One of the central elements of this is the measurement of key ESG characteristics for every fund. While this feels like a prudent approach and allows investors to enjoy a warm glow because their investments are 'doing better', it may be counterproductive.

As evidence of the ESG credentials of their funds, asset managers are increasingly providing a range of relevant metrics. These might be overall ESG scores, or a comparison of the carbon intensity of a fund relative to its benchmark. Although this approach is intuitively sound and is being encouraged by regulators, it is imperfect. Measurement of many ESG factors is incredibly difficult to do well. Assessments of ESG criteria are highly subjective and inconsistent. There is a danger that asset managers simply seek to maximise and manage what can be measured, rather than make investments that might have the largest long-term positive impact on people and the planet.

Carbon is an excellent example of this. Increasingly, funds are reporting on the carbon intensity of their portfolio versus the benchmark, and investors are keen to see that their fund has a lower carbon footprint. Such measures are incredibly limited. Most only cover what are known as scope 1 and scope 2 emissions. Scope 1 emissions are directly from operations (driving a company truck) and scope 2 is energy purchased by the company (for heating and electricity). What is often missed, however, are scope 3 emissions which are in the value chain of the organisation, such as use of the product the company sells. These emissions are regularly overlooked because disclosure is typically poor. Scope 3 emissions can be the major element of a company's carbon footprint. For integrated oil and gas companies, scope 3 emissions will be many times their scope 1 and scope 2 emissions combined.

Measuring scope 3 emissions is complex and intricate, not least because of the double counting – many companies are involved in the value chain of a product, but who is responsible for the carbon emissions? Difficulty, however, does not mean it should be ignored. The danger is that asset managers and investors simply want to prove their ESG characteristics and tick the correct box (particularly from a regulatory perspective); this means that they aim to improve on the benchmark on a scope 1 and 2 basis, and entirely ignore the vitally important scope 3 emissions. A good outcome for the fund but not necessarily the climate.

Focusing only on what can be easily measured and 'proved' is also likely to limit the opportunity and reduce the attractiveness of certain types of companies to fund managers. Take a utility company that is currently reliant on fossil fuels but is embarking on a bold plan to transition to renewable energy. It might be an unattractive investment because its current activities have a negative impact on the ESG metrics a fund manager wants to show their investors, even if what the company is doing will have a hugely positive environmental impact.

The desire of asset managers to capture the ESG investing zeitgeist and ward off fierce competition from index fund providers means the determination to show better ESG metrics is strong. In a complex and emerging area, however, this desire to show proof might undermine the goals of the movement. It is not that measurement and evidence is not important, but we need to be careful of the unintended consequences of the goals that are set.

Asset managers do not rely simply on the wider benefits of ESG investing to attract investors. They can't resist making the case that funds with strong ESG characteristics can generate higher returns, making them better for society, the planet and our profits.

Now that is a powerful story.

Does ESG investing lead to higher returns?

It is inescapable that the growth in ESG investing was boosted by years of strong fund performance. This allowed active managers to build the narrative that we can 'do good' and improve our returns by investing in companies with better sustainability features.

But is this true?

We just don't know.

Simply put, there is insufficient evidence to make claims about the long-term efficacy of investing in companies with better ESG attributes. The performance history of ESG investing was flattered by a decade of staggeringly poor performance from value investing as a style, and outperformance from higher quality and higher growth companies. While accurately defining ESG characteristics may be challenging, it has certainly not been aligned with value investing, which in recent years has come to be defined by old economy, capital intensive stocks, such as mining, and oil and gas. What many present as historic evidence of the performance advantage of ESG investing may be nothing more than a tailwind provided by the general trend of underperformance from unloved and lowly valued investments – not a structural return advantage provided by investing in this fashion.

The time horizon or sample size is not sufficient to make bold claims about the performance of pro-ESG funds. Using similar periods of outperformance, comparable claims were made about technology in the late 1990s and emerging market equities in 2010. Neither ended well.

As we have shown many times in previous chapters, past performance is often a terrible guide to future returns. If we are to make claims about strong future returns we cannot rely on history. We must state the case as to why they will be positive in the future.

Such arguments are rarely made.

The cost of capital conundrum

One of the most common cases around the potential for excess returns from buying stocks with strong ESG features is that they are less exposed to a range of risks in areas such as climate change (environment), labour problems (social) and boardroom malfeasance (governance).

This point about risk might be true and, if it is, should result in a lower cost of capital for the business.

But there is a problem.

If a company carries less risk and the cost of it funding itself is lower, why would this mean higher returns? It would not; it would mean the reverse.

It is often easier to think about this through the eyes of a bond investor. If a company bolsters its balance sheet by selling poorly performing assets and raising cash, we would expect the rate of interest payable on its debt to fall. It is now higher quality; it has reduced the risk of default. Lower risk should equal a lower return.

Some ESG investors seem to think that the lowest risk companies should produce the highest return. Turning capitalism on its head.

There is an argument that as a company improves its ESG credentials and reduces its business risk it should generate higher returns as its cost of capital falls. But most funds now claiming ESG as a crucial part of their process are not saying they are buying weak companies that are getting better. They are saying they are buying good companies and filtering out the bad.

The case that companies with high ESG scores generate better returns must be founded on the idea that they are mispriced (too cheap) either because investors have failed to appreciate how good these companies are or have underestimated how much they will grow. Both are possible but the vast flows into this area in recent years make it somewhat unlikely.

If asset managers are making assertions about the potential return advantage of ESG investing, then they must be clear about how this arises. There are four main paths:

1. **Starting valuations are too low**

   The prices paid now for companies with strong ESG attributes are sufficiently attractive to deliver outperformance through the cash flow provided by current valuation levels. They are more attractively valued than other areas of the market.

2. **Cost of capital is too high**

   Investors are underappreciating the reduced risks enjoyed by sustainable companies, which should be re-priced. Investors should generate profits as their cost of capital falls and valuation increases. The corollary of this is a rising cost of capital for companies with poor ESG credentials.

3. **Growth is underestimated**

   The market is neglecting the long-term growth prospects of many businesses with strong ESG attributes.

4. **Momentum will drive prices higher**

   Stocks in the ESG sweet spot will outperform because of the weight of money and price momentum in this area. Fundamentals are less important than the trend.

It is not enough to talk vaguely about the return advantage of ESG investing; it is critical to be specific about how it is likely to be delivered. What gives it the anomalous potential for higher returns with supposedly reduced risks? If there is no credible explanation, it is no more than another asset manager sales pitch.

We must also accept that the best outcomes for society, might be the worst for investors. For example, what could be better for the growth of renewable energy than a stratospheric investment bubble which sees cheap capital flow into the sector, and huge capacity growth? This would leave many investors nursing heavy losses but be transformative for the global energy mix and increase the potential of meeting climate commitments.

The relationship between ESG investing performance is messy, complex and contradictory, so how should we approach it?

Is ESG investing a good idea?

Although there are areas of concern, the growth in ESG investing is almost certainly a broad positive. The requirement for virtually all asset managers to care about the impact of the companies in which they invest – away from simple shareholder returns – is vital for the environment and society. This does not mean, however, that funds with ESG-centric approaches will deliver superior investment returns.

ESG-orientated funds should not be sold on the basis that they can improve returns. Perhaps some can, but there is simply not sufficient evidence in terms of time or data quality to be sure. As we have already discussed, extrapolating historic fund returns is an incredibly dangerous undertaking for investors, and an ESG label does not remove this risk.

For ESG investing to become truly influential there needs to be an appreciation that the types of return it generates are far broader than that which we typically associate with our fund investments. It is not about headline profits and losses, or performance relative to a particular benchmark, but rather returns that we may never notice.

What does this mean?

There are two types of return from ESG investing, neither of which have anything to do with the performance of a specific fund.

First, the widespread adoption of ESG investing will force companies to improve standards and focus on a wider group of stakeholders. The broad societal benefits of such a movement could be incalculable – if it aids in limiting the rise in global temperatures, for example. This is worth much more than 1% outperformance, but we will never really see it because there is no counterfactual; no parallel universe where these changes did not occur.

Second, our long-term investment returns – in general – may be higher because of the shift towards ESG investing. A disastrous impact from a failure to keep climate change in check will almost inevitably depress returns across many asset classes; thus, the aggregate influence of increased ESG investing may help boost long-run performance of all funds.[14] Again, we will never observe this.

We should not be investing in any given ESG-influenced fund because we expect it to outperform traditional strategies. We should do so because we care about more than simple financial returns, because we believe that the widespread adoption of this approach will improve everyone's returns in the long run. We might even be willing to sacrifice some relative fund performance to achieve it.

What happens when performance deteriorates?

The critical question that every investor in ESG funds should ask is this: what will I do when this style of investing undergoes a spell of weak performance? Could I bear it for six months, one year, what about five years? There are two crucial aspects to remember:

1. Every investment style – no matter how robust – goes through prolonged periods of weak performance. The value factor (buying cheaper companies), one of the most robust investment styles in academic literature, underperformed for over a decade.

2. Styles which have delivered strong results in the recent past are more likely to disappoint in the future. Typically, because the momentum that led them to outperform overshoots, leaving them expensive and likely to revert to mean.[15]

We must disabuse the notion that any investment approach can generate consistently strong results. Our tendency as fund investors to buy outperforming funds and relinquish stragglers leaves an element of uncertainty around the rise of ESG investing. Has its growth really been due to a change in beliefs about corporate responsibility and how companies manage risk, or is this just a cloak for the latest performance fad?

We simply don't know.

Before we invest in an ESG-focused fund we need to ask ourselves how we would feel if the fund we held delivered a positive environmental or social impact but disappointing financial returns.

What is the future of ESG Investing?

We must hope that the commitment from fund investors and asset managers to ESG investing is real and permanent. Asset managers will squabble over definitions, seek to prove that their approach is better than rivals' and make unsubstantiated claims about risk and returns. Investors will be lured into the funds with the most captivating stories and compelling performance. Yet amid the froth, marketing spin and heavy losses in certain speculative areas there may also be a profound change in how companies operate and what investors should expect from them.

The desire to find the best ESG fund misses the point. The move to more sustainable investing practices is about the general, not the specific. The best outcome would be if fund investors no longer have to talk about the subject because the responsibility of companies and asset managers to the planet and its inhabitants has become ingrained behaviour. Not because it sells, but because it is right.

Better outcomes for everyone. The best type of return.

Ten-point fund investor checklist – ESG investing

1. **What ESG issues matter to us?**

   ESG is a somewhat nebulous concept, encompassing a vast range of issues. We should attempt to define the issues that we believe are most important. These could be climate change, biodiversity, workers' rights, or modern slavery. We may then be able to align our fund investing decisions with these priorities.

2. **Does the fund exclude any stocks and industries?**

   The most basic form of ESG investing is excluding companies. There are two reasons for this. The first is moral: we don't agree with the business practice. The second is financial: we believe that the business practice is questionable and this increases the likelihood of poor returns.

3. **Would we be willing to sacrifice returns for better ESG outcomes?**

   It is important to disentangle the performance element of ESG investing with the ESG impact that our investment may have. It is possible to glean how committed we are to ESG investing by understanding whether we would be willing to receive worse fund returns for improved ESG characteristics. Excluding companies must reduce our expected future returns.

4. **Would a fund manager rather a company they own invest in a high return thermal coal project or a low return wind farm project?**

   Although the framing of this question is simplistic, it can provide valuable insights into the priorities of a fund manager.

5. **Is the fund manager utilising voting and engagement productively?**

   When we invest in an equity fund we become part-owners of a range of companies. Our minimum expectation should be that the fund manager votes actively and engages with management on important issues.

6. **Is the asset management firm a signatory to any industry groups or initiatives related to ESG investing?**

The collective power of industry groups and initiatives has the potential to influence significant change.

7. **How would we react to five years of underperformance from ESG-orientated funds?**

ESG-orientated funds will inevitably undergo sustained periods of underperformance. If we are not willing to bear that then we are investing in this area for the wrong reasons.

8. **Do we expect an ESG focus to boost returns? If so, why?**

It is not sufficient to believe that funds with positive ESG characteristics will outperform. We need to have a clear view on what the mispricing is.

9. **Do we understand and trust the ESG metrics being reported on a fund?**

In the rush to prove ESG credentials, many fund managers are utilising metrics with limited merit (such as ESG scores and scope 1 and scope 2 carbon intensity). We should only care about the ESG metrics of a fund if we know what they tell us and that they are meaningful.

10. **Do we want to invest in funds selecting companies that have good ESG credentials now or weaker ones that can improve?**

It is possible that the best results from ESG investing from a returns and impact perspective will be from companies with poor ESG credentials that are improving rather than those that have strong characteristics now. A desire to invest in funds with positive current ESG metrics may actually lead to worse outcomes.

CONCLUSION

WHAT DOES IT take to be an intelligent fund investor? It is certainly not a sophisticated understanding of how global economies function or an otherworldly ability to predict how the stock market will perform over the next six months. It's something different entirely.

Being an intelligent fund investor means holding a sound set of beliefs supported by evidence, and then being able to manage our behaviour. If we can combine those two elements, we can make consistently better investment decisions.

This is easier said than done.

So often our erroneous beliefs and inability to control our behaviour lead to poor choices and costly mistakes. It takes effort to make intelligent decisions about the funds we invest in. This doesn't mean scouring markets for the next great opportunity; in fact it is the opposite. It requires effort to cancel out the incessant noise of financial markets that tempts us away from charting a sensible course.

Intelligent fund investors must understand themselves better than they understand markets.

The chapters in this book are designed to offer a guide to the beliefs and behaviours that will support us in making the right choices to deliver on our long-run goals, while highlighting the dangers and traps that will lead us astray. The topic of each was specifically designed to focus on a critical challenge investors face and how we should approach them. What are the most important lessons to remember?

Chapter 1: when a fund manager is receiving adulation in the media, or all of our friends are buying their fund, it is often the worst time to invest with them. Star status for a fund manager is a warning of problems ahead.

Chapter 2: the rise of low-cost index fund investing has been a wonderful and transformative development for investors. We should not believe, however, that the typical approach adopted by index funds – to allocate by market capitalisation weights – will always be successful. History suggests there will be periods when alternative approaches find favour. We should be prepared for such scenarios.

Chapter 3: our aversion to the pain of losses and discomfort when experiencing fund volatility means that we are drawn towards funds that exhibit smooth performance. The serene trajectory of these funds often makes us negligent to the risks lurking below the surface of calm waters.

Chapter 4: complex funds promise the world – the ability to deliver strong returns in all market conditions and significant diversification from traditional investments – but so often they disappoint. Not only that, they break a crucial rule that should be applied by all investors: never invest in something we don't understand.

Chapter 5: investors adore stories. Stories make chaotic and unpredictable financial markets seem simple and even exciting. The problem is that the more compelling the narrative, the more likely we are to make bad decisions.

Chapter 6: volatility has become the pre-eminent measure of risk in the investment industry, but the real risk that investors face is failing to meet their long-term objectives. This risk can be realised in two ways: a rapid disaster caused by injudicious decisions such as a lack of diversification, or slow disappointment from the compound impact of small costs and mistakes.

Chapter 7: the investment decisions of most fund investors are dominated by past performance. We invest in funds that have outperformed in recent times and relinquish the laggards. Although this is a strategy that makes us feel good in the moment, buying winners and selling losers is the worst possible approach to fund selection and will come with severe long-term costs.

Chapter 8: most asset managers are incentivised to maximise short-term inflows and profits, which means they market the latest investment fads, attempt to sell funds with unsustainably strong performance and rarely close funds to new money even if the investment approach is compromised. Fund investors should assume that their incentives are not aligned with the asset manager with which they are invested. Even schemes such as performance fees, which are designed to provide better alignment, fail to serve that purpose. A new model is needed.

Chapter 9: the ability to adopt a long-term approach is the one true advantage that all fund investors hold. It allows us to benefit from the hidden force of compounding and gives us a fighting chance of separating the luck and randomness of financial markets from investment skill. There is no greater challenge than having the behavioural discipline to be a long-term investor, but there is also no greater reward.

Chapter 10: ESG has become the defining feature of fund investing in recent years and its rapid growth has made it difficult to separate meaning from marketing. There are genuine and profound benefits to all investors of a broad shift towards a form of capitalism that is more considerate towards all stakeholders, but to discover this we need to look through the industry sales and spin.

The decisions we make about the funds we invest in really matter. They will play a huge role in defining our financial future. If we can combine sound beliefs with a willingness to understand our own behaviour, then we really can be intelligent fund investors.

ACKNOWLEDGEMENTS

A couple of years after I started my blog – behaviouralinvestment.com – Craig Pearce approached me about writing a book. I was very excited by the idea but had no comprehension of the chasm between producing a collection of 800-word blog posts and creating a coherent and compelling book. This became vividly apparent when I submitted my first draft chapter, not a trace of which you will find in the pages before you. Suffice to say that *The Intelligent Fund Investor* would not be in existence without guidance and feedback from Craig and the team at Harriman House, to whom I am indebted.

The contents of *The Intelligent Fund Investor* have been influenced and shaped by so many individuals it will be impossible to list them all. It bears a vast collection of fingerprints, and I am thankful for all those unbeknownst contributors.

I am particularly grateful to Robin Powell, Harry Holzer and Rory Maguire, who all took time to provide invaluable feedback on draft versions.

There are certain people who have had a direct and profound impact. They are:

My parents, for giving so much to provide me with opportunities in life.

Andy Evans, with whom I undoubtedly spent more time considering the ideas and concepts in this book than any other person. If you are planning to write a book, I would heartily recommend discussing it regularly with someone smarter than you.

My wife, Natalie, not only for being an incredibly patient and talented proof-reader, but also for her unwavering support and love. To quote a certain Jane Austen novel: "What do I not owe you!"

Thank you

ENDNOTES

Introduction

1 'Neil Woodford: The Man Who Cannot Stop Making Money' *BBC News Online* (19 June 2015).

Prologue

1 Chang, T. Y., Solomon, D. H., & Westerfield, M. M. (2016). 'Looking for someone to blame: Delegation, cognitive dissonance, and the disposition effect' *The Journal of Finance*, 71(1), 267–302.

Chapter 1

1 'Woodford fund breaches unquoted limit after Guernsey delistings' *FT.com* (31 July 2019).

2 'Woodford and partner took £13.8m dividend in run-up to fund crisis' *The Guardian* (7 January 2020).

3 Taleb, N. *Skin in the Game: Hidden Asymmetries in Daily Life* (Random House, 2020).

4 Kroll, M. J., Toombs, L. A., & Wright, P. (2000). 'Napoleon's tragic march home from Moscow: Lessons in hubris' *Academy of Management Perspectives*, 14(1), 117–128.

5 'Anthony Bolton: "The Chinese are great liars"' *Citywire* (1 April 2014).

Chapter 2

1 www.morningstar.co.uk/uk/news/210970/active-funds-fail-the-test-in-2020.aspx

2 Anadu, K., Kruttli, M., McCabe, P., & Osambela, E. (2020). 'The shift from active to passive investing: Risks to financial stability?' *Financial Analysts Journal*, 76(4), 23–39.

3   Clare, A., Motson, N., & Thomas, S. (2013). 'An Evaluation of Alternative Equity Indices – Part 2: Fundamental Weighting Schemes' *Cass Consulting*; Clare, A., Motson, N., & Thomas, S. (2013). 'An Evaluation of Alternative Equity Indices – Part 1: Heuristic and Optimised Weighting Schemes' *Available at SSRN 2242028*.

4   'SPIVA U.S. Scorecard 2021' *S&P Dow Jones Indices*.

5   'SPIVA Europe Scorecard 2021' *S&P Dow Jones Indices*.

6   'The Cyclical Nature of Active and Passive Investing' *Hartford Funds* (2021).

Chapter 3

1   'Life Settlement Funds' *Investment Week* (28 January 2008).

2   'FCA to Ban the Sale of "Ponzi"-like "Death Bonds"' *Citywire.co.uk* (28 November 2011).

3   'FCA Warns on Toxic Life Settlement Funds' *FT.com* (28 November 2011).

4   'Traded Life Policy Investments' *FCA.org.uk* (18 April 2016).

5   'Suspended EEA Life Settlement Fund overvalued by $100m, Says Auditor' *Money Marketing* (3 July 2013).

6   Shiller, R. J. (1980). 'Do stock prices move too much to be justified by subsequent changes in dividends?' (No. w0456). National Bureau of Economic Research.

7   'Has the Government Really Hit 100,000 Tests Per Day, and What Happens Next' *fullfact.org* (1 May 2020).

8   'McKinsey's Private Equity Annual Review' *McKinsey* (24 March 2022).

9   'A New Equilibrium: Private Equity's Growing Role in Capital Formation and the Critical Implications for Investors' *Kenan Institute of Private Enterprise* (16 October 2019).

10   Phalippou, L. (2020). 'An Inconvenient Fact: Private Equity Returns & The Billionaire Factory' *University of Oxford, Said Business School, Working Paper*.

11   Chingono, B., & Rasmussen, D. (2015). 'Leveraged Small Value Equities' *available at SSRN 2639647*.

12   'Time to Embrace Private Equity' BNY Mellon Wealth Management (Accessed 3 June 2022)

13   Halpern, D. *Inside the Nudge Unit: How Small Changes Can Make a Big Difference* (Random House 2015).

Chapter 4

1   'Fidelity Bans Retail Investors from Trading Short Volatility' *FT.com* (9 February 2018).

2   'Credit Suisse Defeats Lawsuit Over Huge US Volatility Crash' *Reuters.com* (25 September 2019).

3   'The Costly Fallacy of "Asset Class" Investment' *FT.com* (18 October 2020).

4   Perrow, C. *Normal Accidents*. (Princeton University Press 2011).

5 'Hedge Funds, Leverage and the Lessons of Long-Term Capital Management' *Report of The President's Working Group on Financial Markets* (28 April 1999).

6 Ennis, R. M. (2020). 'Institutional investment strategy and manager choice: A critique' *The Journal of Portfolio Management*, 46(5), 104–117.

Chapter 5

1 'Building Better Global Economic BRICS Goldman Sachs Global Economic Paper No:66' (30 November 2001).

2 'A Rough Ride on BRIC Road' Gregg Wolper. Morningstar.com (19 March 2013).

3 'Bloody Ridiculous Investment Concept (BRIC) revisited' Albert Edwards. *SG Global Strategy Weekly* (19 July 2013).

4 Taleb, N. *Fooled by Randomness: The Hidden Role of Chance in Life and in Markets* (Random House, 2005).

5 Tetlock, P. *Expert Political Judgement: How Good is It? How Can We Know?* (Princeton University Press, 2017).

6 Storr, W. *The Science of Storytelling: Why Stories Make Us Human and How to Tell Them Better* (Abrams, 2020).

7 'ETFGI reports assets invested in Thematic ETFs and ETPs listed globally reached a record US$394 billion at the end of February 2021' *ETFGI.com* (24 March 2021).

8 Ben-David, I., Franzoni, F., Kim, B., & Moussawi, R. (2021). *Competition for Attention in the ETF Space* (No. w28369). National Bureau of Economic Research.

9 Pennington, N., & Hastie, R. (1992). 'Explaining the evidence: Tests of the Story Model for juror decision making' *Journal of Personality and Social Psychology*, 62(2), 189.

10 Martin, S and Marks, J. *Messengers: Who We Listen To, Who We Don't, and Why* (Random House 2019).

Chapter 6

1 'The Pursuit of Extreme Returns' Baillie Gifford (Quarter 1, 2018).

2 Bessembinder, H. (2018). 'Do stocks outperform Treasury bills?' *Journal of Financial Economics*, 129(3), 440–457.

3 'Major Valeant Shareholder Sequoia Exits Its Stake After Losses' *fiercepharma. com* (13 July 2016).

4 'Valeant: The Harder They Fall' *FT.com* (28 March 2016).

5 'How Seqoia Fund's Valeant Mistake Upended a Top Performance' *Bloomberg. com* (20 April 2016).

6 Tsai, C. I., Klayman, J., & Hastie, R. (2008). 'Effects of amount of information on judgment accuracy and confidence' *Organizational Behavior and Human Decision Processes*, 107(2), 97–105.

7   Slovic, P. (1973). 'Behavioral problems of adhering to a decision policy'

8   'Quantifying the Impact of Chasing Fund Performance' *Vanguard* (July 2014).

9   Cornell, B., Hsu, J., & Nanigian, D. (2017). 'Does Past Performance Matter in Investment Manager Selection?' *The Journal of Portfolio Management*, 43(4), 33–43.

Chapter 7

1   Goyal, A., & Wahal, S. (2008). 'The selection and termination of investment management firms by plan sponsors' *The Journal of Finance*, 63(4), 1805-1847.

2   Bailey, D. H., & De Prado, M. L. (2014). 'The deflated Sharpe ratio: correcting for selection bias, backtest overfitting, and non-normality' *The Journal of Portfolio Management*, 40(5), 94–107.

3   Bailey, D. H., Borwein, J., Lopez de Prado, M., & Zhu, Q. J. (2014). 'Pseudo-mathematics and financial charlatanism: The effects of backtest overfitting on out-of-sample performance' *Notices of the American Mathematical Society*, 61(5), 458–471.

4   Huang, S., Song, Y., & Xiang, H. (2020). 'The Smart Beta Mirage' available at SSRN 3622753.

5   'How Data (And Some Breathtaking Soccer) Brought Liverpool to the Cusp of Glory' *New York Times Magazine* (22 May 2019).

6   Biermann, C. *The Science and Art of a Data Revolution* (Kings Road Publishing, 2019).

Chapter 8

1   'The Great Hanoi Rat Massacre: A Conversation with Michael G. Vann' *Made In China Journal* (20 August 2020).

2   Vann, M. G. (2003). 'Of rats, rice, and race: The great Hanoi rat massacre, an episode in French colonial history' *French Colonial History*, 4(1), 191–203.

3   'The Great Hanoi Rat Massacre of 1902 Did Not Go As Planned' *Atlas Obscura* (6 June 2017).

4   Akerlof, G. A. (1978). 'The market for "lemons": Quality uncertainty and the market mechanism' *Uncertainty in Economics* (pp. 235–251). Academic Press.

5   'Rokos hedge fund made £900m profit in early days of pandemic' *FT.com* (4 January 2022).

6   'Orbis Isn't Afraid to Refund Fees for Poor Performance' *Bloomberg.com* (19 January 2021).

7   'These Fund Managers Are True Believers' *Morningstar* (18 November 2020); Khorana, A., Servaes, H., & Wedge, L. (2007). 'Portfolio manager ownership and fund performance' *Journal of Financial Economics*, 85(1), 179–204; Ma, L., & Tang, Y. (2019). 'Portfolio manager ownership and mutual fund risk taking' *Management Science*, 65(12), 5518–5534.

Chapter 9

1 Berkshire Hathaway Inc. Shareholder Letter 2021.

2 'The Folly of Hiring Winners and Selling Losers' *Research Affiliates* (September 2017).

3 'Firing Warren Buffett' UBS CIO Global Blog (13 March 2019).

4 'Patience with Active Performance Cyclicality: It's Harder Than You Think' *The Journal of Investing* (June 2021).

5 Bar-Eli, M., Azar, O. H., Ritov, I., Keidar-Levin, Y., & Schein, G. (2007). 'Action bias among elite soccer goalkeepers: The case of penalty kicks' *Journal of Economic Psychology*, 28(5), 606–621.

6 Simon, H. A. (1956). 'Rational choice and the structure of the environment' *Psychological Review*, 63(2), 129.

7 Peng, S. (2013). 'Maximizing and satisficing in decision-making dyads' available at repository.upenn.edu/cgi/viewcontent.cgi?article=1101&context=wharton_research_scholars.

8 Schwartz, B. (2000). 'Self-determination: The tyranny of freedom' *American Psychologist*, 55(1), 79.

9 Roets, A., Schwartz, B., & Guan, Y. (2012). 'The tyranny of choice: A cross-cultural investigation of maximizing-satisficing effects on well-being' *Judgment and Decision Making*, 7(6), 689.

10 Granovetter, M. (1978). 'Threshold models of collective behavior' *American journal of sociology*, 83(6), 1420–1443.

11 Sunstein, C. R. (2002). 'Probability neglect: Emotions, worst cases, and law' *The Yale Law Journal*, 112(1), 61–107.

12 'Crisis Investing I: How to Maximise Returns During a Panic' *Verdad Capital* (10 February 2020).

Chapter 10

1 'Record Flows Pour Into ESG Funds as Their "Wokeness" is Debated' *Bloomberg. com* (25 October 2020).

2 'BP Set to Pay Largest Ever Environmental Fine in US History for Gulf Oil Spill' *The Guardian* (2 July 2015).

3 'Revealed: The 20 Firms Behind a Third of All Carbon Emissions' *The Guardian* (9 October 2019).

4 www.bp.com/en/global/corporate/who-we-are/our-ambition/our-aims.html.

5 'Countries Fossil Fuel Production Plans Inconsistent with Paris Agreement' *Climate Change News* (20 November 2019).

6 Friedman, M. (2007). 'The social responsibility of business is to increase its profits' *Corporate Ethics and Corporate Governance* (173–178). Springer, Berlin, Heidelberg.

7   'Total Chief Warns of Renewable Energy Bubble' *FT.com* (17 February 2021).

8   'Cambridge University to Divest from Fossil Fuels by 2030' *The Guardian* (1 October 2020).

9   'Church of England Pulls Out of Fossil Fuels, But Where Does It Invest its Cash?' *The Independent* (1 May 2015).

10 'Divesting Fossil Fuels Has Zero Climate Impact, Says Bill Gates' *FT.com* (17 September 2019).

11 '2021 Progress Report' Climate Action 100+ Group.

12 'Blackrock, Vanguard Show Little Favor for Shareholder ESG Votes' *Bloomberg.com* (1 January 2020).

13 'ESG Ratings Key Issues Framework' *MSCI.com* (16 June 2021).

14 'Investing in a Time of Climate Change' *Mercer* (2019).

15 'If Factor Returns Are Predictable, Why is There an Investor Return Gap?' *Rayliant Advisors* (18 November 2015).

ABOUT THE AUTHOR

 Joe Wiggins has worked in the mutual fund industry since 2004, holding senior portfolio management and fund selection roles at some of the UK's largest asset and wealth managers. He is the author of the successful investment blog: behaviouralinvestment.com. Its distinctive focus on investor behaviour and decision making has reached a worldwide audience. He is a specialist in behavioural finance and in 2017 completed a Master's degree in Behavioural Science at the London School of Economics, for which he received the Brian Abel-Smith prize for outstanding performance.

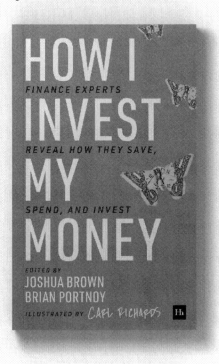
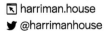

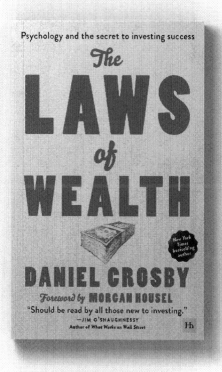
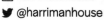

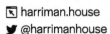